Harry J. Truman

I0078534

Ten Habits of the
Spiritually Tough

Faith Development for the
Twenty-first Century

Racketty-Packetty Press   Kendallville, IN 46755

Harry J. Truman has most recently served as pastor to

the First Presbyterian Church of Kendallville, Indiana,

and was ordained into the pastoral ministry in 1990.

In over twenty-five years in ministry, he has staffed

five congregations and one retirement community.

Truman is a graduate of both Albion College (BA)

and Pittsburgh Theological Seminary (MDiv).

Ten Habits of the Spiritually Tough is his first published book.

Racketty-Packetty Press, Kendallville, IN 46755

© 2016 by Harry J. Truman

Printed in the USA and around the world by CreateSpace

24 23 22 21 20 19 18 17 16   1 2 3 4 5

ISBN-13: 978-0-9970125-0-7 (paperback)

Library of Congress Control Number: 2015957081

This paper meets the requirements of ANSI/NISO Z39.48.1992 (Permanence of Paper)

Front cover illustration is "The Conversion of Saint Paul"

by Jacopo Tintoretto, 1518 - 1594, c. 1545, and is reprinted with

permission from the National Archives, Washington DC,

Samuel H. Kress Collection.

For my wife Darlene, because she has demonstrated

to me what real patience looks like.

Table of Contents

Preface

If we walk the aisles of the religion section in our local large-chain book store, we might see any number of titles which include some form of the word spirituality in them. Spirituality has been a popular topic to write and to read about for a while now — not just Christian spirituality, but spirituality across every belief domain we can name.[1] This book is not another in a continued series of feel-good tracts on Christian spirituality. If you are doing some browsing and have picked up this book thinking it is perhaps about spirituality, put it back on the shelf immediately lest you find yourself exposed to ideas you hadn't intended to encounter.

The previous sentence was — by the way — a joke. What is no laughing matter is that if a person delves into this book, he or she will find a cluster of ideas which together add up to one greatly overlooked concept in the faith-life of most people of faith and especially Christians: toughness. It is the premise of this book that toughness is a quality lacking in the majority of professing followers of Jesus of Nazareth in the twenty-first century. I am not suggesting the Church is filled with millions of professing wimps, I am flat out accusing it of being so.

This book is a painful but necessary corrective to the crisis of faith being experienced by millions of current and former believers. It is a crisis of faith borne in large measure from a reliance on an illusionary power called spiritual strength.[2] This I find to be both unfortunate and ironic. It is unfortunate because our journey through this existence is difficult enough without making it more so by willfully disregarding the single, most-guaranteed way of increasing our ability to endure life's hardships. Especially where Christians are concerned, it is ironic because Jesus Christ was the toughest person ever to walk the face of the earth. You would have thought his followers would have picked up on this quality by now.

Over twelve chapters, the reader will discover ten vital habits which can toughen up his or her faith-life thus making possible the overcoming of hardships which otherwise would have affected their relationships with both loved ones and with God. At the same time, these habits are designed to keep the reader more humble in her or his walk with the Lord.

I am calling these abilities "habits" because, whether good or bad, habits are actions broadly accessible to most people. And that is an important truth to hold onto because too many of us believe the qualities which enable us to endure hardships are beyond our reach. Reading this book should go a long way to dispelling this false notion.

Illuminating these habits will be profiles of people both from the pages of the Bible and from our contemporary world. Their examples can teach us about spiritual toughness in ways which a dry, academic discussion could never accomplish. Human beings from diverse eras were able to be spiritually tough in the face of life's hardships. If they could do it, then so can we.

I have met or have known people who, in every other aspect of their walk with God, are capable of amazing acts of witness to the Gospel — except when some tragedy enters the picture. Then, their faith evaporates like a badly formed argument. It reminds me of the adage, "His devotion to the cause was a mile wide but an inch deep."[3] However, if we toughen up our faith-life, we also deepen our devotion to God.

Some people may get upset as they read this book because it challenges anyone who believes in the value of spiritual strength by stripping away all pretense we have been trusting God if we have been attempting to be stronger in our faith. For me, writing this book was the faith development equivalent of going from one fad diet to another only to discover that all along I should have been eating less and exercising more. In reading this book, you may discover something similar for yourself. Now, if you are game, I challenge you to continue reading.

Harry J. Truman

Kendallville, IN

January 14, 2015

1

Strength vs Toughness

What is Wrong with Spiritual Strength?

What is wrong with spiritual strength? Nothing at all is wrong. Nothing, except that no person of faith you or I have read about, heard about, or personally have known has it. I will grant you this is a harsh and uncompromising statement. A more diplomatic way of putting it would be to say that when God's people do have spiritual strength, it is both fleeting and underwhelming. Harshness and diplomacy aside, here is the most theologically honest picture of what I'm talking about:

"The Lord looks down from heaven on the children of man, to see if there are any who understand, who seek after God. They have all turned aside; together they have become corrupt; there is none who does good, not even one" (Psalm 14:2-3 ESV).[1]

The cold, hard truth of the matter is this: none of us is strong. And I don't mean just in terms of our spirituality. I mean in every aspect of our lives. Some of us may be physically, mentally, or psychologically stronger than the person next to us, but even that advantage is no match for the kind of power arrayed against us in this life. Even folk who possess above-average strength are barely strong enough to be considered weak:

"For the foolishness of God is wiser than men, and the weakness of God is stronger than men" (1 Corinthians 1:25).

Consider that among the people who went through Hurricane Katrina or Super Storm Sandy, there had to be the full spectrum of ability represented from the very weakest of individuals to the very strongest. Now, if being strong is supposedly a valuable asset in a time of crisis, how did any weak people survive those calamities whereas some strong people did not? The answer is obvious: Surviving hardships takes qualities additional to that of strength. Obviously there is a certain randomness of survivability contained within any tragic event — what some people other than myself might call luck — but a quality consistently found within people who are able to survive hardship is mental toughness. A book entitled "Lifespan Perspectives on Natural Disasters" edited by Katie E. Cherry is but one source among dozens which bears out this truth.[2]

It logically follows that what is true about our lives in general should also be true about our faith-lives in particular: toughness matters more than strength. Let us at least be honest with ourselves; the amount of spiritual strength we want to have is far less than we will ever have. Have any of us moved a mountain lately? Certainly I haven't and I don't think you have either. When it comes to our faith-lives, we just can't do the kind of heavy lifting we would like to believe we can do. The problem, of course, is sin. Sin fatally weakens our spiritual strength and there is no power in this world able to alter this truth.[3]

Sin is to every human being what kryptonite is to Superman. On his home planet, Clark Kent would have been just a normal person. If we were transported to a world without sin, we would be more than able to leap tall buildings with a single bound or go move a mountain or two. That is, we could do these things if sin was a condition which existed outside of us. But because sin is embedded within our humanity, we can't help but to carry this fatal flaw with us wherever we go.[4]

Sadly, we all live on Planet Earth. Well, now, hold that thought. I probably don't know you, so for all I know, you don't believe in sin or that you are a sinner. If this is the case, then you don't live where I or the rest of humanity lives. In order for a person to believe himself to be strong and his spiritual strength to be all he needs to carry him into heaven, that person must live on a fantasy planet like Krypton. If this describes your mind-set, well, about all I can say is you can stop reading this book now because what follows is clearly going to be a waste of your time. This is a book on faith development for people who live on Planet Earth.

Strength in any form — but especially in the form of achievement — is a persistent illusion.

In most societies, people are encouraged to explore the limits of human achievement. This is one aspect of the world's strength-language which gives energy to the efforts of every athlete and entrepreneur, every performer and politician. Westerners and people from Asian cultures in particular will often strive until they either succeed or quite literally die in the attempt.[5] Absent strength-language, there is no worldly achievement. A serious problem arises, however, when we believe the attainment of God's kingdom is just one more goal in a long line of possible earthly endeavors. It isn't.

And as wonderful as worldly accomplishment is, it often feeds strength-language's first illusion. When we succeed in forging some achievement, and then we continue to do so, we sometimes fall victim to believing we got to where we are by our own steam. This is called hubris. Hubris is for successful people what sleight-of-hand is for the magician's audience: a mis-direction designed to trick the mind.

Even a free-styling solo rock climber doesn't get to the top of the mountain by himself or herself. Behind those strong efforts are trainers and mentors and the combined efforts of countless others. It turns out very

3

few human achievements are truly forged in isolation. This awkward truth doesn't stop some men and women from taking solitary credit for what they are able to do. We have all seen, heard about, or perhaps been guilty of the sin of hubris. To be celebrated for some achievement is a temptation few of us can resist. We like to imagine ourselves as being strong, ready-for-anything people. Our sinfulness, however, creates a distorted self-image. The painful truth is that the power of achievement can become an illusion.

Hubris can also affect nations. The belief in collective strength is behind every great societal achievement from the building of the Egyptian pyramids to the Apollo Program. Nations have great power and sometimes that collective strength is even used for the betterment of humanity. However, the illusion of strength is just the same. It doesn't change just because we are talking about a million people instead of one. Nations also may fall victim to the same over-optimistic image which distorts reality for an individual.

In ancient Rome, a "triumphator" being feted with a crown representing his victory in battle was, at times, accompanied on his chariot in a parade through Rome by a slave whispering in his ear, "*a memento mori*," (you are yet to die.)[6] It is the mortality of individuals and the nations they create which serves as the basis for the second illusion where strength and strength-language are concerned: the idea our creations can withstand the ravages of time. If the earth's continents have been made and remade, crumbled into dust, melted and spewed forth again, what right do any of us have in hoping our achievements will last? And if our achievements cannot last, then in what sense do we have any enduring strength?

The truth of our achievements being far less individually created — coupled with the twin conditions of our sin and mortality — sweep away any and all pretense of human strength. Still, we have been living under this persistent illusion for a long time, and many of us are quite happy to go on doing so.

It is no wonder we've bought into this illusion.

We must not blame ourselves too much for being fooled by this illusion. For our entire lives, we have been taught to think, speak, and act using strength-language[7]. From sacred spaces to secular halls, many prominent voices have been telling us we need to be stronger. Variations on this theme include admonitions to be faster, prettier, more wealthy, smarter — you get the picture. Just about every authority figure we have ever encountered from our parents and our teachers to pastors and sports figures speaks this language. They do this because strength-language is what human beings have spoken at least since the days of Noah:

"Now the whole earth had one language and the same words. They said, 'Come, let us build ourselves a city and a tower with the top in the heavens, and let us make a name for ourselves'" (Genesis 11:1, 4).

If this sounds familiar, it is because we have heard this story time and again down through the ages. Manifest destinies and master races are but two possible points on this spectrum of the human desire for more worldly strength and power. The people who built the Tower of Babel imagined themselves to be invincible. And the illusion of the boundless nature of their abilities has not waned in their children and grandchildren down to this present time. To be in this world is to exist in a vast arena of achievement and failure. And in this forum, strength and the language which gives birth to it reign supreme. Now, why is that?

Strength is sexy whereas toughness is... what, exactly?

Spider-Man was my favorite superhero growing up. Even at my age, I still hold a soft spot for the old wall-crawler. People all over the world like their superheroes. I have already mentioned two of them. There are dozens more because chances are we will find one who resembles us, and, so our thinking goes something like this: "If I can't be strong, at least Spider-Man or Wonder Woman can be."

And don't we love to see our heroes in action! Strength and the projection of power is sexy, and exciting, and fun, and you name it, but whatever it is, we love it. Strength fills theater seats. It sells millions of books every year. But, here is something to chew on: The bad guys in these stories are always looking for ways of overcoming the superhero's power. They almost never succeed, but not because the man or woman in the red, white, and blue tights is strong. Something other than the hero's superpowers usually wins the day.

There is this fellow from the pages of the Bible who typifies what I am talking about. You might remember him from that one day you didn't spend day-dreaming in Sunday School. That is because chapters 13 through 16 of Judges are some of the most exciting Bible passages you may have read. Still can't place him? He is the hero with the hair — long, gorgeous locks which gave him his fantastic strength:

"But his father and mother said to him, 'Is there not a woman among the daughters of your relatives, or among all our people, that you must go to take a wife from the uncircumcised Philistines?'" (Judges 14:3)

(Like many of us, this man's weakness was his attraction to physical beauty.)

"But Samson said to his father, 'Get her for me, for she is right in my eyes'" (Judges 14:3).

Samson ends up marrying the girl, but the story of their union ends badly for just about everyone. Then, this strong-man compounds his weakness by failing to learn from his mistake. When Delilah discovers his hair to be the source of his power, that spells the beginning of the end for good old Samson. In a final act of desperation, he prays to God for one last spasm of strength to avenge his tormentors. God grants the request and everyone dies when Samson collapses the house around their ears.

The point I am making is this: Even superheroes like Samson can lose their strength. But, they only become truly imperiled when they lose their toughness. Samson's toughness — like Wolverine's or The Hulk's — was more important to him than his strength. The same is true for us, but the irony is we have a difficult time seeing this because toughness is often obscured by the seductive qualities of strength. This happens because strength involves power going in the correct direction — according to the world's strength-language. Let us now focus on that.

Vectors of power: strength vs toughness

Strength and toughness are both examples of power-in-action. In fact, they are often confused with one another. While similar in many respects, they differ in terms of the vector (direction) in which that power flows. The power of strength is more valuable — so the world wants us to believe — because the vector of power begins within us and is projected outward. The power of strength is inherently aggressive. It is very often violent, destructive, intimidating, and intentional.[8] The power of strength fills multiplex cinema seats on Saturday evening and mega-church pews on Sunday morning. The projection of strength can frighten us unless it is we ourselves doing the projecting. It is this fundamental quality of strength which makes it addictive, dangerous, and seductively seem more important to us than toughness.

But toughness, too, is a kind of power. The difference is this: Toughness is the ability to absorb the power of something or someone

7

else's strength. Toughness is inherently defensive. It is protective, reflective, and deflective. The ability to absorb the punishing power of something else's strength can also be exhausting and even demoralizing. Only a masochist becomes addicted to toughness. And for reasons like these toughness is less valued by us than is strength.

Nonetheless, it is the premise of this book that toughness is a far more important quality to possess than strength. And when it comes to our faith-life, spiritual toughness is a rock-solid foundation whereas spiritual strength is an illusion. Here are the apostle Paul's thoughts on the subject:

"Finally, be strong in the Lord and in the strength of his might.[9] Therefore take up the whole armor of God, that you may be able to withstand in the evil day, and having done all, to stand firm. Stand, therefore, having fastened on the belt of truth, and having put on the breastplate of righteousness, and, as shoes for your feet, having put on the readiness given by the gospel of peace. In all circumstances take up the shield of faith, with which you can extinguish all the flaming darts of the evil one; and take the helmet of salvation, and the sword of the Spirit, which is the word of God" (Ephesians 6:10, 13-17).

Paul's idea of strength comes from our ability to endure. He has us wearing the uniform and equipment of a soldier: helmet and body armor and boots all designed to protect us against power projected from Satan or worldly adversaries. The Christian's only offensive weapon is God's word provided through the Holy Spirit. Followers of Jesus Christ are to be dressed for battle for defensive more so than for offensive purposes.

Spiritual toughness is what Paul is referring to when he speaks of the "strength" of the Lord's might. Paul's goal is to train up the faithful to overcome by withstanding. Our counter-strike comes in the form of the truth. That is all. No projection of worldly power; no fighting fire with fire. Now, the quality essential to achieving this victory is toughness. Why is this the case? Because the last one standing is usually the tougher of the two combatants — usually, but not always.

Most of us by now have heard about the 300 Spartans at Thermopylae. Perhaps Paul was thinking of them, too, when he wrote those words I quoted from his letter to the Ephesians. It is said these Greeks saved Western civilization. How? It wasn't because they were stronger than the Persians — they weren't. They all died. But, those Spartans were some tough soldiers. They absorbed a ton of punishment and made it possible for other Greeks to ultimately prevail over Xerxes I, his son, and grandson.[10] This brings us to another quality of toughness: its tendency to be sacrificial. But hold onto that thought for a while — we will come back to it later.

Spiritual toughness can be and, in fact, must be learned.

Anyone can learn how to be tough. Just ask Teddy Roosevelt. Obviously, we can't actually speak to the man right now since his area code and location are a bit out of our reach. But, we can read about him. And, if we were to open Doris Kearns Goodwin's biography "The Bully Pulpit," we would discover TR described himself as a "timid" child.[11] He had to purposefully mold himself into the tough-as-nails Rough Rider, environmentalist, and politician we love to hear about. For Roosevelt, it came down to practicing over and over again the right techniques until learning how to be tough became being habitually tough. For example, Goodwin tells us it took Roosevelt over two years of boxing just for him to make a "perceptible improvement."[12] As an adult, our 26th President took that mental attitude and applied it to every aspect of his life. In fact, Goodwin reminds us TR was so tough he once took a bullet in the ribcage from an assassin and kept on orating![13]

But before we begin learning how to become tougher in our faith-life, there are some things we must unlearn. Specifically, we are going to have to stop thinking, speaking, and acting using the world's strength-is-my-friend language. As I have stated previously, strength has its place in the world. But, when it comes to our faith-life, strength-language is a bankrupt philosophy.

When we reach out for God using spiritual strength we end up with a fistful of disappointment every time. In fact, reliance on the world's strength-language is a likely reason why so many Christians lapse in their faith. They try to use spiritual strength in their faith-walk only to discover they never seem to have enough of it. It then becomes only a matter of time until repeated futility leads such people away from the Church. It is the type of disappointment the apostle Peter learned about the hard way:

"But immediately, Jesus spoke to them, saying, 'Take heart; it is I. Do not be afraid.' And Peter answered him, 'Lord, if it is you, command me to come to you on the water.' He said, 'Come.' So Peter got out of the boat and walked on the water and came to Jesus. But when he saw the wind, he was afraid, and beginning to sink, he cried out, 'Lord, save me!'" (Matthew 14: 27-30)

It takes some kind of power to walk on liquid water. Peter had it — for all of a few moments. This is what I meant when I said earlier our spiritual strength is both fleeting and underwhelming. Spiritual strength is a persistent illusion which remains intact so long as we forget about our sin, our mortality, and our interconnectedness to God and people.

The world is actively helping us to forget about these things every day. We must not forget, because when we do, we immediately fall victim to the worst kind of spiritual sleight-of-hand. If we, like Peter, want to have a deeper faith-life with the Lord, we must learn how to become spiritually tougher instead of spiritually stronger. And if we are to have any hope of doing this, we must forge the courage to embrace change. It is the first habit of the spiritually tough we are going to encounter.

2

Habit #1: Have the Courage to Embrace Change

If we can't or won't embrace change, then God has little use for us.

Time and again throughout Scripture, God sets aside, protects, and uses people who are willing to embrace change.[1] Those people who tend to be stiff-necked God usually just pounds into oblivion. Sometimes, those he uses and the stiff-necks are one and the same person. One thing the Bible teaches is that, in this life, our immovable, obstinate wills are no match for the Almighty's overwhelming force.

Here is another way of saying it: either we adapt, or we fade away. We adapt by learning how to embrace change. We fade into irrelevance before God when we refuse to do so. It is just that simple. It's also biblical. By way of example, please consider what are among the first words we hear from both John the Baptist and Jesus of Nazareth. Let us hear the Gospel of Mark tell us:

"John appeared, baptizing in the wilderness and proclaiming a baptism of repentance for the forgiveness of sins" (Mark 1:4).

"The time is fulfilled, and the kingdom of God is at hand; repent and believe in the gospel" (Mark 1:14-15).

Repenting is the first, most important quality Jesus and John the Baptist were looking for in people who desired to become citizens in God's kingdom. Ok, so, "What is repentance?" you may ask. I will tell you, but in Greek. Repentance in the English language is equivalent to the Greek word μετάνοια (pronounced: metá-noi-a).[2] In the context of our faith-life, it means to turn around or turn away from sin, but in its every-day usage μετάνοια simply means to change one's mind about something.

So, based on this understanding, the first thing John and Jesus do is to go around Judea and Galilee telling the populace they must reflect about their faith-life, turn aside from the current way they have been relating to God, and follow a new path to salvation. To do this is to respond positively to the gospel of Jesus Christ... what Christians call the Good News.

Well, this seems easy enough, right? "Change is as good as a vacation," so the saying goes. John and Jesus put out the call, and the Jews change both their minds and their ways. Uh... not so much as we find out when we read the New Testament. Few Jews changed anything about themselves. Even Jesus' own disciples had a difficult time with this. It took them standing in the midst of his resurrected body before this understanding took hold. Why was that? Well, it turns out embracing change takes a specific emotional skill: courage. Until that moment in the upper room on the third day after the death of the Lord, Jesus' disciples didn't have much courage.

We all know what courage is: it is taking some action in spite of being afraid to do it. And just to be clear, few of us ever truly overcomes a particular fear. Just ask any veteran of any battle from any war, and they will say how little they trusted their fellow soldiers who claimed to have no fear in the face of hostile fire.[3] Your typical soldier is scared to death every time he or she puts that weapon to their shoulder and looks down the barrel knowing somewhere down-range is an adversary doing the same damn thing.

Non-veterans may well wonder how such a person is able to function. Soldiers do so by learning how to accommodate their fear even to the point of using it to motivate themselves and other soldiers around them. This learning begins in basic training as raw recruits are exposed to live weapons fire at close quarters. And this training continues to be applied to them, layer upon layer like a lacquer, until the day they put that training to the test on a field of battle and their real training begins! Plus, most of us would rather die than disappoint a family member. And that is what a platoon of soldiers on a battlefield is: a family.

In the area of our faith-life and especially as it pertains to how we relate with God, courage often takes the form of God asking someone to do something difficult and that person does it. For example, God tells Noah to build an ark big enough to hold mated pairs of every creature on earth. In agreeing to do this, Noah defies every bit of conventional wisdom. He goes against all logic and reason, and incurs the ridicule and anger of his neighbors. But none of that matters to Noah as much as his devotion to God. Noah was one courageous person and a fine role model for faith, but I'd rather focus on another patriarch we encounter in the book of Genesis: Abram. Here was his task:

"Now the Lord said to Abram, 'Go from your country and your kindred and your father's house to the land that I will show you'" (Genesis 12:1).

For us, this can be done without too much hassle. It is never an easy thing to pick up and move our families. And as I know from personal experience, even a short move can be difficult. But, we have rentable trailers and professional moving companies. Some of us even have expense accounts. We have good roads and even better maps. Finally, you and I usually know the place on that map where the journey ends.

Abram had none of those things to rely on. All he had was the courage to trust God's command. Abram and Sarai walked with their servants and their animals from Ur of the Chaldeans (a place about 200 miles south of Bagdad, Iraq) to Haran in present-day Syria, to Shechem (an area located in the northern part of the West Bank between Israel and Jordan). Abram had the courage to embrace a huge amount of change. Because of this, God called Abram, protected him and Sarai and made him the father of multitudes. This is why Abram/Abraham is such an important example for Christians, Jews, and Muslims when it comes to their faith-lives. He is rightly lifted up as an example of someone who lived by faith:

"No distrust made him waver concerning the promise of God, but he grew strong in his faith as he gave glory to God, fully convinced that God was able to do what he had promised. That is why his faith was counted to him as righteousness" (Romans 4:20-22).

Seeing courage as a virtue does not help us.

Maya Angelou is credited with writing, "Courage is the most important of all the virtues because without courage, you can't practice any other virtue consistently."[4] And ancient minds as varied as Plato, Cicero, and St. Augustine all elevated courage into the pantheon of virtue.[5] But, does believing courage to be a virtue help us if, by labelling it thus, we keep it on some dusty pedestal there little-used and under-appreciated?

Consider, also, that if our understanding of courage is too lofty, then we may find ourselves in the impossible position of believing we first need courage in order to go after it! While this seeming paradox can provide some people with a ready-made excuse to not pursue courage, even a modest application of logic is enough to expose this conundrum as false. Since we can witness, on a daily basis, people acting with courage, it must be a quality quite near to us.

And this is good because for courage to be learnable by us, I believe it first must be accessible to us. Courage becomes accessible to us the moment we imagine ourselves displaying it to ourselves and others. So, go ahead and pull down courage from its marbled perch. Look for and make opportunities to practice being courageous until it becomes habitual. Practicing courage is straight-up facing what we are afraid of. In the context of this chapter, that means accommodating ourselves to the uncomfortable condition we call change.

We have been facing change all our lives. In fact, we were born to experience change.

Perhaps we know change by other names: growth or maturation. Maybe the fact this condition sticks to us like our shadow has lulled us into forgetting it is even there. Believe me when I say I completely understand. Most of the time, I don't track the changes in my life any better than you do. For human beings, change is something which just happens whether or not we want it to.

"And Jesus increased in wisdom and in stature and in favor with God and man" (Luke 2:52).

Even our Lord was subject to this condition. When the apostle Paul says in Philippians 2:7 that Jesus was "born in the likeness of men," he is also including the human trait of changing over time. The phrase "in wisdom and in stature" from Luke's Gospel encompasses all aspects of Jesus' personality from the physical to the mental to the psychological and everything which defined our Lord's material existence.[6]

Everything about us changes over time. We begin helpless and, if we live long enough, end up right back there being cared for by the hands of other people. And in between those book-ends is the story which tracks how we have grown and matured... or not. We have all heard the phrases, "The more things change, the more they stay the same" and "Change is the only constant." Both ideas exist to express in words the mysterious inner transformation which is our birth-right as recipients of this gift we call life.

In the realm of physics, change is expressed as the tendency for all things to drift toward a state of increasing disorder. The technical term for this process is entropy.[7] Translated from its Greek origins, entropy means "inner transformation" in English. Now, the problem with both entropy and our conventional wisdom about change is we have no way to determine if these things are, in fact, true. Until the universe's existence ends, the jury is out on entropy. And it could just as easily be true that even change changes. All we know for certain is we are swimming in change and unable to climb out of the pool.

This is why I didn't express this habit as "the courage to change." It takes no courage to change. What it does take is to get out of bed every morning. Change, as I said, happens whether or not we want it to. Now, here's another problem: Often we don't like the changes which sneak up and bite us on our back-sides. These sort of changes seem too-often birthed in tragedy; like getting a phone call from out of the blue informing us a relative has died unexpectedly. (Really, though, even an expected death is a difficult change to endure.)

God created this beautiful world; he set the earth to orbit around the sun; and he filled the world with all manner of life. Lastly, he molded people in his own image and placed them in a garden to care for his vast creation. From that moment on everything about that creation changed — constantly. And as Jesus' brother reminds us in the following passage, there is nothing we can do about it:

"Come now, you who say, 'Today or tomorrow we will go into such and such town and spend a year there and trade and make a profit,' yet you do not know what tomorrow will bring. What is your life? For you are a mist that appears for a little time and then vanishes" (James 4:13-14).

Embracing change is the most important everlasting life skill we need to learn while in the world.

We exist in a world of change not to fight against this condition but to learn from it. The experiences we accumulate in this life are our great teachers — if we are student enough to pay attention to the lessons being offered. And whether we go through every academy of hard knocks or take our studies under shade trees in sylvan glades encapsulated by blue skies we are expected to draw some wisdom from the experience.

When I first entered Pittsburgh Theological Seminary, the president at the time, C. Samuel Calian, told our class the most important things we would learn during our time there were things about ourselves. He spoke the truth. The same thing is true for every pupil enrolled in the Creator's school of change.

This is why we must develop the courage to embrace change instead of merely tolerating it or, heaven forbid, ignoring it. When we pass up the opportunity to embrace some changing aspect of the world around us or even within us, it is one less chance to acquire a skill which is far more important for us to have than anything else in our lives. Think I am just blowing smoke? Well, then, think on this:

"I tell you this, brothers and sisters: flesh and blood cannot inherit the kingdom of God, nor does the perishable inherit the imperishable. Behold! I tell you a mystery. We shall not all sleep, but we shall all be changed, in a moment, in the twinkling of an eye, at the last trumpet" (1 Corinthians 15:50-52).

The apostle Paul reveals this to anyone who wants to know: There will come a day when humanity will be subject to the final change when God strips all sin (and previous change) from us and makes us to be as holy and as changeless as he is. But, I guarantee we won't be included in this event unless we have already learned how to embrace change. It is something faithful people do. We are living in this world to prepare for the day of the "last trumpet." Face up to it. Don't diminish your opportunity for heavenly glory by embracing only those changes which seem easiest to accept.

Facing our fear of change takes practice.

Earlier, I used President Teddy Roosevelt as an example of how we can learn to be more courageous. Here is something else Doris Kearns Goodwin uncovered about this idea:

"As a childhood friend [of Roosevelt's] observed, 'by constantly forcing himself to do the difficult or even the dangerous thing,' he was able to cultivate courage as 'a matter of habit, in the sense of repeated effort and repeated exercise of will-power'"[8] [bracketed words are mine].

You and I — like TR and his friend — can learn how to be unafraid. Of course, by unafraid, I mean we are able to accommodate our fear to something more important. In the case of a soldier's fear, it is the welfare of his or her comrades and the success of the mission. In the case of the people of God — people like you and me — it is often for similar reasons.

Who among us would not spring into action if we saw a toddler about to be hit by a car? Anyone with both the ability and the opportunity would do it. More often than I care to recall, I have been among the first people at the scene of a traffic accident. On one occasion, my wife and I witnessed the collision of a semi rig and a John Deere tractor hauling two bins of grain.

Now, I react badly to the sight of blood. I might even pass out if I saw you bleeding; it is that bad. But, as soon as my wife slowed down our van sufficiently, I was out the side door and running over to the point of impact. Amid the smell of leaking fuel and a smashed and smoking engine, myself and this other man pried open the driver's door on the semi and pulled the driver from his cab. He was a busted-up, bloody mess. At that moment, however, the two of us were on a mission, and fear for our personal safety or my particular attitude about the sight of blood were nowhere on the scene.

Remember, I said we all have trouble tracking the changes we have been through. If I were a betting man, I would lay down some coin you are already tougher than you think you are because you are also more courageous than you think you are. Somewhere along the way, we all acquire a measure of an ability to accommodate our fear to some higher purpose. We just need to remember those moments and use them to practice being courageous until we are habitually courageous.

When it comes to facing our fear, we must focus on the mission. This was the ability the resurrected Jesus gave to his friends. Our mission as people of faith is to place front and center in our minds the welfare of those more in need than we are. Every time sin and doubt begin to nip at us, we need to remember that one, clear call from the Bible which remains seared into our minds:

"So, whatever you wish that others would do to you, do also to them, for this is the Law and the Prophets" (Matthew 7:12).

The so-called Golden Rule can be our key to unlocking the courage to embrace the change we are already in the midst of. Let us not listen to the world's strength-language which keeps telling us to wage war against the changes all around us or to ignore them when we decide we can't prevail against them. Let us not seek to selfishly conserve a strength we don't really have or, in fact, need. It is far more important for us to be tough: to endure; to overcome by withstanding; and to counter-strike the power of our adversaries by speaking truth.

In the context of this chapter, it has meant embracing change and accommodating our fears to God's higher purposes for us. It also means we must surrender the thought we are in control of anything in this life. It is less about taking charge of each new day and more about managing its circumstances. This is the second habit of the spiritually tough and the focus of the next chapter.

3

Habit #2: Learn How to Manage Life

Strength-language is also the language of control.

The same people who have been telling us our whole lives to "be stronger and smarter and wealthier and prettier" are also the ones urging us to: "Take control of your life!" On the surface, this sounds like good advice. Taking control of our life is a powerful idea; it is the responsible thing to do and seems intuitively to be the right thing to do as an adult.[1]

As way of analogy, let us compare taking control of our lives to driving a car. Learning how to drive is like being in our adolescent and teenage years. Passing the driving test, getting that license, buying insurance and a car: These things are all rites-of-passage to adulthood which culminate with us sitting down behind the steering wheel, buckling in, turning on the ignition, putting the vehicle in gear, and driving off into the bright sunrise of a new day. It certainly sounds right.

Too bad it isn't. Here is why this analogy doesn't hold up: We understand the operations of an automobile well enough to control our car in almost all driving conditions. On the other hand, we don't understand how we ourselves are supposed to function (let alone why we do what we do) on a typical, stress-free day. What we do not understand, we can

21

hardly be expected to control. I absolutely love the convoluted way the apostle Paul expresses this frustration:

"For I do not understand my own actions. For I do not do what I want, but I do the very thing I hate. Now if I do what I do not want, I agree with the law, that [the law] is [correct]. So now it is no longer I who do it, but sin that dwells within me. For I know that nothing good dwells within me, that is, in my flesh. For I have the desire to do what is right, but not the ability to carry it out. For I do not do the good I want, but the evil I do not want is what I keep on doing" (Romans 7:15-19) [bracketed words are mine].

As soon as our heads stop spinning, we can pause, take a deep breath, and agree with Paul: this is, in fact, the daily condition under which we also strive. We like to believe we have control of our lives and are quick to offer this advice to young people, but the sad truth is: We just can't control what we do not understand. Furthermore, Paul flat out says the sin within our physical bodies thwarts any hope of control. That is one grim truth.

So, where do we begin to refute this false idea surrounding our need to control? What I mean is: The world is such a large canvas and this book just one, small paint brush. How are we going to cover layer upon layer of dried up, useless, old paint and wallpaper which forms the facade of this entrenched mind-set? Maybe we should begin by going in the other direction.

After my grandmother Truman sold her home and moved into a smaller apartment, I was asked by the young couple who bought her place to help them remove the kitchen wallpaper. Did I mention my grandmother had lived in a farmhouse which was, in the 1970s, already over one hundred years old? Yeah, it had *that* many layers of stuff on the walls! It took us forever (or at least as much time as forever is to a fifteen-year-old boy) to scrape and sand our way back down to the plaster.

This is the same kind of effort needed here. But stripping away innumerable layers of control-minded attitudes from our heads is not just difficult; it is damned exhausting! And to top it off, if you are anything like me, chances are this is one habit of spiritual toughness you are

22

reluctant to attempt to learn let alone to master because you are stymied by the concept of surrender.

Nobody likes to surrender. It is a word we don't want in our lexicon, let alone a choice stalking us at every turn. And here I am asking we volunteer to give up our all-too-human, very compelling need to control. I understand just how difficult this might be for some of us. Reading the first two chapters of this book hasn't broken you from thinking, speaking, and acting using the world's strength-language. Well, writing about it probably hasn't cured me of this attitude either. Then again, maybe it has, and that would be great. But, I doubt it, so let us proceed as if we are both still hooked on this drug called "the need to control." The problem has been around for a while:

"...but some of them went to the Pharisees and told them what Jesus had done. So the chief priests and the Pharisees gathered the Council and said, 'What are we to do? For this man performs many signs. If we let him go on like this, everyone will believe in him, and the Romans will come and take away both our place and our nation'" (John 11:46-48).

Every time I read these words, I feel a deep sadness for those Jewish leaders. This is the very picture of desperation, isn't it? Jesus' ministry is putting them in a terrible bind. On the one hand, if he keeps on performing miracles and undermining their authority, the Romans will get rid of them and probably begin the direct rule of their nation. On the other hand, if they themselves get rid of Jesus, their Jewish subjects might just get rid of them.

The Sanhedrin was trying to maintain control in a situation where they had none. They were caught between forces they did not create and could not influence. Like people in a wagon careening down a hill, they were just along for the ride. If these men were like most people in a similar situation, they secretly knew just how little control they had but projected to outsiders the exact opposite. Now, honestly, haven't most of us done the same thing? How different might these seemingly hopeless situations be if — instead of feeling like we needed to control events — we chose to manage them.

During the early months of World War II in Europe — just prior to and after the British were forced into a humiliating retreat at Dunkirk — it fell upon RAF Chief Air Marshall Sir Hugh Dowding to develop a strategy of sustaining Great Britain's air-war effort against German aggression. In spite of intense political pressure to focus on the production of bombers, Dowding strongly advocated for an increase in the number of single-seat strike fighters. For his efforts his superiors in the Air Council demoted him to take charge of the newly created RAF Fighter Command.[2] It was this propitious decision which made possible Dowding's later tactic of managed attrition against the Luftwaffe's 3-to-1 superiority in number of aircraft:

"With a clairvoyance exceeding that of his fellow air marshals, let alone of his government, Dowding had a good picture in his mind of the battle to come, and what it would take to win."[3]

What it would take was for Great Britain to absorb a large amount of damage from German bombers, and for Fighter Command to obscure their relative strength against the Luftwaffe by never defending against an attack with anything greater than squadrons. Dowding knew England would get a bloody nose in the coming fight; but also that if she, as it were, could turn her cheek enough times, the German air assets would be worn down.

The resulting strategy has been called by historians The Battle of Britain. By September 15, 1940, the Luftwaffe was made to concede defeat in its desire to control English airspace because RAF pilots in their Hurricanes and Spitfires were just too tough to vanquish — although the "permanence" of this "victory" was not immediately understood.[4]

Individuals and groups who make decisions using strength-language will always use that way of thinking in an attempt to control events. People who rely instead on their toughness will opt to manage those events as best they can. Remember, no matter the conflict or hardship, our toughness usually outlasts someone else's strength.

Nevertheless, most of us mature into our adult years being told to *carpe diem* our way to success. The desire to be strong and the need to seize the day are two facets on the same jewel. And, boy-oh-boy, doesn't that diamond twinkle in the light of day! Aren't strength and control so desirable and so powerful? And don't we all salivate at the thought of being in command of our lives enough and being strong enough to join the ranks of the elites?

Remember, though, diamonds are valued as much for their toughness as for their sparkle. In fact, I would argue a diamond's toughness is the quality which makes possible its enduring value. As enticing at it might appear to us, the need to be in control of our lives is the losing strategy. Like spiritual strength, it is a phantom philosophy. Now, there is someone in control of our lives. It is just not us, and it doesn't have to be sin.

God is the Captain of our fate.

"And the Lord said to Moses, 'See, I have made you like God to Pharaoh, and your brother Aaron shall be your prophet. You shall speak all that I command you, and your brother Aaron shall tell Pharaoh to let the people of Israel go out of this land. But I will harden Pharaoh's heart'" (Exodus 7:1-3).

This snippet from one of the Bible's great dramatic confrontations brings into focus something as true for us today as it was for Moses, Aaron, Pharaoh, and the million-plus Israelites: God is in control of our lives. The God of Abraham, Isaac and Jacob directed Moses to go back into Egypt, Aaron to speak to Pharaoh, and Pharaoh to have his heart become hardened to the pleas of the Israelites so that not only would he fall, but fall hard. Could God have secured the release of the Israelites without crushing Pharaoh and the Egyptians? Of course, but the admonition to, "Let my people go!" was only half the story. In fact, Moses and Aaron's mission to speak truth to power wasn't even the most important part of this story.

Communicating to everyone God alone is in control of human history is the point of the Israelites' flight from Egypt. The first part of this lesson is conveyed through the crushing of the Egyptians, the second part in the crushing of the Israelites' will in the desert. Only when the truth of God's control becomes burnished into their hearts and minds are the Israelites ready to take possession of the Promised Land.

God often places in our path opportunities for us to be brought low to remind us our control of anything is like our strength: fleeting and underwhelming. It, too, is an illusion; and something about which Jesus had to remind both the Jews and even his own disciples:

"It is easier for a camel to go through the eye of a needle than for a rich person to enter the kingdom of God. And they were exceedingly astonished, and said to him, 'Then who can be saved?' Jesus looked at them and said, 'With man it is impossible, but not with God. For all things are possible with God'" (Mark 10:25-27).

The disciples believed — as many people still do — that wealth equates with having control over one's fate. But while riches often make living in this world a bit easier, there is no connection between wealth and control. In fact, King Solomon reminds us the opposite is more often the case:

"He who loves money will not be satisfied with money, nor he who loves wealth with his income; this also is [an illusion]. When goods increase, they increase those who eat them, and what advantage has their owner but to see them [vanish before] his eyes?" (Ecclesiastes 5:10-11) [bracketed words are mine]

If it is true (as the words to that famous Beatles' song go) "Money can't buy you love," then it certainly can't buy us control. And if wealth can't buy us control, then nothing can. Rich or poor, all of us would do well to keep in mind this simple truth: God is the Captain of our fate. The best we can hope for in this life is to be like Sir Hugh Dowding during the Battle of Britain and manage the daily events which confront us.

We can't surrender something we have never had. This is why the focus is on our need to control.

There is a contemporary female athlete who knows quite a bit about falling hard and about the illusion of being in control. Her name is Lindsay Vonn, and, as I am writing these words, she has just achieved another championship in downhill skiing. In 2013, Ms. Vonn fell on a Super-G race course in Austria and shattered a bone in her left leg and tore ligaments in her right knee. But, after many months of rehabilitation and training, she is back at the top of her sport.[5]

As with every other competitor she faces, I must believe Lindsay Vonn is pumped by the speed of skiing. The desire to win and forge a new world record is also present. It would be impossible to believe Ms. Vonn goes out onto a slope thinking she is going to lose control. No athlete ever steps onto the field of competition with such an attitude.[6]

But the truth is, whatever control an athlete has in her given sport is narrowly held and easily lost... especially if she loses concentration. But, concentration, skill, and even raw athletic ability cannot guarantee control. Competitors like Lindsay Vonn get to the top of their particular sport because they are able to thrive better and manage the chaos of the moment more skillfully than those around them. Retired professional golfer Jack Nicholas captured this idea well when he said, "A lot of guys can go out and hit a golf ball, but they have no idea how to manage what they do with the ball."[7] Being able to manage the field of play — not controlling it — is the secret to an athlete's success.

I imagine Vonn and Nicholas have no illusions about any of this: in a contest between themselves and their respective courses laid out before them, the physical elements cannot be controlled, only managed. Both competitors merely navigate whatever conditions nature throws at them. In a sense, neither Nicholas or Vonn is even in competition with their fellow athletes, but with their own ability to handle the elements, their own anxiety, and that rush of adrenalin. Well, this same winning formula is available to you and me as we navigate the ups and downs of our own lives. Here is the essence of what I'm talking about:

"But whatever anyone boasts of — I am speaking like a fool — I also dare to boast of that... Are they servants of Christ? I am a better one — I am talking like a madman — with far greater labors, far more imprisonments, with countless beatings, and often near death. Five times I received at the hands of the Jews the forty lashes less one. Three times I was beaten with rods. Once I was stoned. Three times I was shipwrecked; a night and a day I was adrift at sea" (2 Corinthians 11:21, 23-27).

The apostle Paul's litany of his personal hardships on behalf of preaching the gospel reads like some kind of sick joke. What he was able to accomplish, however, was no laughing matter. He started countless churches; wrote most of the epistles we read in the New Testament, and penned some of the most elegant and iconic verse we are wont to recall. Paul did what he did because he surrendered his need to control his life. He endured all that hardship not because he was stronger than other evangelists but because he was tougher! He had the courage to embrace the profound change which captured him on the Damascus Road. Because of all this, he transformed the people he met with God's message of sacrificial love through Jesus Christ. And what made all this possible? Here is Paul's winning formula:

"So, to keep me from becoming conceited because of the surpassing greatness of the revelations, a thorn was given me in the flesh, a messenger of Satan to harass me, to keep me from becoming conceited. Three times I pleaded with the Lord about this, that it should leave me. But he said to me, 'My grace is sufficient for you, for my power is made perfect in weakness.' Therefore I will boast all the more gladly of my weaknesses, so that the power of Christ may rest

upon me. **For the sake of Christ, then, I am content with weakness, insults, hardships, persecutions, and calamities. For when I am weak, then I am strong"** (2 Corinthians 12:7-10).

If great achievers like Sir Hugh Dowding, Lindsay Vonn, Jack Nicholas, and the apostle Paul all understood they were not in control and were even willing to give up the need for it, then so too can we surrender our need to control. And we had better do it sooner rather than later because the need to control is toxic to us, and destructive to those people closest to us.

The need to control is a powerful drug which poisons our relationships.

It is bad enough for us personally when we labor under the illusion we need to take control of our lives. This problem is greatly amplified when this need for control spills over into someone else's life. Remember reading this before?

"Judge not, that you be not judged. For with the judgment you pronounce you will be judged, and with the measure you use it will be measured to you. Why do you see the speck that is in your brother's eye, but do not notice the log that is in your own eye?" (Matthew 7:1-3)

Or, how about this passage from Paul's Letter to the Romans?

"Who are you to pass judgment on the servant of another? It is before his own master that he stands or falls. And he will be upheld, for the Lord is able to make him stand" (Romans 14:4).

Our tendency to be judgmental flows directly from the illusion we are strong and know what we are doing. This is yet one more sad consequence of using the world's strength-language to try to fuel our faith in God. But, if someone close to us is a professing Christian, Jesus, we are told, has the privilege and responsibility of judging them. Therefore, read this and repeat, please: "It is not my job to judge or, by any other means, seek to control the lives of those people closest to me."

Like shampoo, we need to rinse and continue to repeat this sentence until all residue from that extra-strength, control-minded language washes away from our heads. And, even if a person isn't a Christian, the same thing holds true. A person's status (believer or unbeliever) doesn't change the fact God is in control. God made the universe and everything in it, so he gets to decide our fate. Not us. Not sin. God.

Now, I understand the need to control others is often an even more addictive habit than focusing this desire for control on ourselves. We often learn this bad habit after having failed to control our life but before realizing we should be managing it instead. What also plays into this mind-set is our inability to detect God's hand guiding our lives in any good way. What we are left with is the very frightening sense that if we do not fill this void, no one will. And since we have been thinking, speaking, and acting using strength-language, we try to take control of whatever situation needs fixing.

We can hardly be blamed. All this control and strength energy has to go somewhere.

Many of us reading these words and understanding for perhaps the first time the depth of damage we have been doing to our loved ones by seeking to control their lives are probably feeling guilty about now. I know what this feels like and — believe it or not — it is actually a good place to be. If this is you, then congratulate yourself for getting this far. Now go find a kitchen timer and set it for five minutes. Really, I am not kidding. Set the blasted thing for five minutes. You have that long to live with your guilt. When the timer goes off, you need to be done feeling sorry for yourself. Go on, this book can wait.

Why am I saying this? There are two reasons. The first one is this: guilt exists to stop us in our tracks and make it easier for us to turn — to change our minds — away from this dried up, useless mind-set of the need to control ourselves or others. Once guilt has accomplished this task, hanging onto it is pointless. (Also, consider this: regret is just one more concept which flows from strength-language.) The second reason harkens back to something I said earlier in this book: we have been raised in and continually bathed in this toxic attitude our entire lives. Those who forced this strength and control belief-system on us — and continue to reinforce it — bear the greater burden of guilt.

Now that we understand as perhaps never before why we have felt compelled to be one of those control freaks everybody dislikes, we can begin to embrace the change to a different way of relating to the world, to those closest to us, and especially to how we relate to God. We do this by first remembering God is in control of our lives; not our sins and certainly not us. Once we believe this, we will discover it to be much easier to manage the events of our lives instead of trying to wrestle them into submission.

Then we need to find a purpose important enough to make it worth us accommodating our fears, igniting our courage, and surrendering our need to control. We will discover this purpose when we begin to covet God's call to us. That is the next habit of the spiritually tough.

4

Habit #3: Covet God's Call

To covet something is to desire it beyond all rational thought.

There are stories in the Bible involving someone expressing an intense desire to the degree considered covetous.[1] Unfortunately, none of them have God as the object of that desire. Often, it's about a man wanting a woman:

"It happened, late one afternoon, when David arose from his couch and was walking on the roof of the king's house, that he saw from the roof a woman bathing; and the woman was very beautiful. And David sent and inquired about the woman. And one said, 'Is not this Bathsheba, the daughter of Eliam, the wife of Uriah the Hittite?' So David sent messengers and took her, and she came to him, and he lay with her" (2 Samuel 11:2-4).

After David forces Bathsheba into an affair, he then conspires to get rid of her husband by making Uriah lead a military charge designed to get him killed. Uriah — not aware of the king's rape of his wife — eagerly

32

obeys David's command and honorably dies so that David may continue his dishonorable relationship with Bathsheba. It isn't until the prophet Nathan brings to David God's judgment on the matter that the king repents. But, his tears and pleadings are not enough to save the child produced from this shameful union.

If we live with the twin accolades of success and celebrity long enough, the temptation to believe we are invincible — or at least above the law — begins to set in. Next thing we know, we have gone and done some bone-headed thing like King David did with Bathsheba.

Now, if some tawdry tale from the dustbins of history seems passé, we need go only as far as the daily newspapers or the latest webcasts to see examples of human covetousness in action. Russia wants the Crimea, so Putin takes it. ISIL wants a new caliphate in the Middle East, so it heaps misery upon a region already made miserable by conflict. Actor 'A' wants a divorce from Entertainer 'B' so that he/she can get together with Celebrity 'C'. Corporations want to maximize profits at the expense of workers' wages. Politicians want to destroy the opposing political party more than they want to pass meaningful legislation. Smokers want to smoke, drinkers want to drink and everybody wants the government out of their bedrooms. It is a sad truism of human nature: Most of us want what we want when we want it.

Behavioral psychologist Lawrence Kohlberg identified three distinct levels of human moral judgment, each having two stages. The first level he termed "Preconventional." Children operating within this level see the world "...in terms of the physical power of those who enunciate the rules and labels."[2] They also can ask themselves what they might be able to get by doing something their friends or parents want them to do. This is usually the age at which it becomes possible to negotiate with a child an allowance in exchange for chores completed. It is a relatively immature realm of ethical development. We certainly weren't meant to remain in it for the entirety of our lives.

Kohlberg saw the higher expressions of ethical behavior as embedded within the third level of moral judgment which he described as "Postconventional, Autonomous, or Principled." It is here where a person's ethics become governed by universal principles of right and wrong. The sixth stage is where he or she is able to decide that where a particular law violates universal ethical principles, "… one acts in accordance with the principle" rather than with the law.[3]

Employing Kohlberg's typology, it is clear to me there are millions of adults in the world with their moral judgment stuck within that first level. Most of them are speaking strength-language and actively seeking after more power. Too many of them are armed to the teeth and will never be satisfied with what they currently possess. And here we thought all along the novel "Lord of the Flies" was a work of fiction.[4] Silly us!

This juvenile and toxic attitude lays like a rabid dog at the base of every theft, rape, assault, murder, and war of aggression. It exists in every word of political bluster and in every syllable of threatened violence. And it has been this way since human beings were kicked out of the Garden of Eden because all covetousness not directed at God is fueled by strength-language. It is strength-language which tells a person, "Might makes right!" It seeps into our souls and tricks us into thinking, "I am powerful enough to take what I want without regard to those weaklings in my way!"

In a philosophy called by its detractors "Social Darwinism," nineteenth-century sociologists such as Thomas Malthus, Francis Galton, and Herbert Spencer attempted to apply Charles Darwin's observations about biological selection to societal systems. This kind of twisted thinking — including Friedrich Nietzsche's concept of the *Übermensch* — reached a crescendo within Nazi Germany when Adolph Hitler bent these ideas into a state-sponsored version of covetousness directed to territorial and economic gain all under the feigned rationality of modern science.[5]

Under this ideology, cohorts, corporations, and cabals give as justification for crushing their enemies the rationalization that only the strong are permitted to survive. It is this vacuous, self-centered morality which becomes the answer to the question of why there is so much misery in the world. Our sin is fueled, in large measure, by the world's strength-language which leads too many of us to arrest our moral judgment at the stage where self-interest reigns supreme. Said another way, we covet things apart from God because our lack of moral sophistication binds us to do so. And, this self-imposed, arrested ethical maturing is literally driving us insane. As sweet as they are, most ten-year-old children are incapable of thinking or acting rationally. Sadly, neither are their adult counterparts.

The spiritually tough person, however, understands it to be far more important — and in every way measurable, healthier — to seek after a moral framework which contains universal truth, the locus of which is found in Almighty God instead of in themselves. At the heart of this moral framework is God's personal call to service.

Being bound to God's call to service frees us from bondage to the world.

Tyron Edwards — a nineteenth-century American theologian and grandson of Jonathan Edwards — is responsible for two of the most insightful observations on a person's faith-life. One of them is this:

"Thoughts lead on to purposes; purposes go forth in action; actions form habits; habits decide character; and character fixes our destiny."[6]

He is completely correct, of course. Habits do decide our character. It is one of the reasons why I feel so driven to write this book. Only devils have the habits of a devil and saints the habits of a saint. The habits of human beings fall somewhere in between. One thing is certain, however: If we direct our thinking toward God's eternal truths and turn away (repent) from our desire for self-interest, we stand a far better chance of actually hearing the Almighty speaking to us. Our Heavenly Father is constantly calling out to us to go and do something for him. The prophet Jonah understood what I am saying:

"Now the word of the Lord came to Jonah the son of Amittai, saying, 'Arise, go to Nineveh, that great city, and call out against it, for their evil has come up before me.' But Jonah rose to flee to Tarshish from the presence of the Lord" (Jonah 1:1-3).

Not that we are always good at obeying God's call to service. But this doesn't stop God from reaching out to us. Jonah eventually got the hint the Lord was serious about him going and preaching to the people of Nineveh. First, however, all of Jonah's wants had to be digested (as it were) in the belly of a great fish. In my case, I am pleased to say God didn't have to go quite that far, but he, nonetheless, subjected me to some pretty difficult circumstances before he succeeded in grabbing my attention. He must still, from time to time, remind me who is in charge!

Chances are if we are experiencing difficulty in our lives, this is God giving us the opportunity to draw close enough to him so we may hear him calling us to come serve him. Hardships are *not* punishments from God. (If someone has told you this, they have told you an untruth and you should question their advice.) Hardships are, however, painful moments designed to get us to stop punishing ourselves. We each punish ourselves in unique ways, but they all begin in the same place: we have volunteered to be enslaved by the world.

The history of salvation is the story of God claiming for himself a people who are to be a nation of priests willing to proclaim to the rest of humanity God's gospel of love. The incident in the Old Testament called the Exodus is the tale of a million Israelites going through some very difficult days, hearing the voice of God through Moses, and yet who still are unable to keep from punishing themselves. Below is but one example of what I mean:

"All the congregation of the people of Israel moved on from the wilderness of Sin by stages, according to the commandment of the Lord, and camped at Rephidim, but there was no water for the people to drink. Therefore, the people quarreled with Moses and said, 'Give us water to drink.' And Moses said to them, 'Why do you quarrel with me? Why do you test the Lord?'" (Exodus 17:1-2)

I would love to say it is an easy thing for us to stop punishing ourselves, but that would be a lie. It is damned hard to do! In fact, if your life experiences are anything like the Israelites or mine, becoming freed from the world's grip will entail the following: 1) stop doing whatever bone-headed thing it is you are doing; 2) carefully pull your proverbial head out of your proverbial ass, so that; 3) you can begin to more clearly hear what God is saying to you.

That second task is obviously the most painful thing to do, but, nonetheless, we all have to do it. Call it eating crow or humble pie, but we have to get real about taking responsibility for our sins. In the context of our building up habits of spiritual toughness, taking responsibility begins by acknowledging we have been speaking and trading and working in strength-language for far too long. It also means we admit to being sinners.

Well, the time has come for us to cease our grumbling about how harsh our taskmaster the world is and to begin listening for and trusting in God's call to freedom through service. The thing is, we have to want this freedom to serve God beyond all rational thought.

After taking ownership of our sins, the next step is to discover how we are to serve God.

One of the most valuable habits of spiritual toughness is found in acquiring an irrational love for God. We begin to do this when we ask the very basic question, "What does God require of me?" The answer to this question was given to Moses just after the death of his brother Aaron and after he had spent forty days and nights listening to God:

"And now, Israel, what does the Lord your God require of you, but to fear the Lord your God, to walk in his ways, to love him, to serve the Lord your God with all your heart and with all your soul, and to keep the commandments and statutes of the Lord, which I am commanding today" (Deuteronomy 10:12-13).

Buried right in the heart of Israel's call to service is the admonition to love God. Put simply: We cannot discover how we are to serve God unless we are first willing to love God. Sin, we have learned, causes us to do this imperfectly. Even so, let us continue with this truth in mind as we look at what it means to seek out God's call.

Coveting God's call to service, as I have said, begins when we give ourselves the opportunity to more clearly hear what he might be saying to us. Now, I should point out God rarely speaks to us directly. It is more often the case he communicates how we are to serve him by two specific means: personal skills and obstacles.

Personal skills — also called gifts of the Spirit — are things we discover about ourselves as we embrace the change which happens as we mature into adulthood. Every human being without exception is given some unique set of abilities. They are talents we must choose to use in God's service or not. Obstacles are things we encounter in life when our particular gifts of the Spirit are not being used in God's service. They are quite literally opportunities for us to redirect those abilities toward God's will and purpose for us.

In order to be led by God's call to service, we must understand both our gifts of the Spirit and the obstacles we encounter for what they actually are: blessings from God he expects us to use to honor him. We misuse these gifts whenever we get it into our heads these abilities are there solely for our benefit or that the obstacles are there to punish us.

Probably like you, I also have made the mistake of treating God's blessings with a fierce selfishness. We really have no one to blame but our sinful selves: We simply cannot accomplish what God requires of us with any effort approaching perfection. In my case, it was because I chose to love worldly things more than God.

38

Universal truth is found in God's call for us to love both him and our neighbors.

In the context of this book on faith-development, repentance means to stop speaking, thinking, and acting using strength-language. We must turn away from the self-centered ways in which we have been organizing our life up to now. We must also then turn to God with an attitude of irrational love. And if we are able to do this, that is a good thing. But, it doesn't mean we have begun to covet God's call to service. That takes something more. It takes focusing our minds on and surrendering our way of thinking to universal truth.

And, as far as truth goes, it is literally God's way or the highway. The answer to Pontius Pilate's question of, "What is truth?" is to say truth is whatever God says it is.[7] We do not get to define this concept, because this is what we were doing when we were organizing our lives around our narrow self-interest and performing our actions based upon the habits of spiritual strength. So, before we can begin to covet God's call-to-service, we need to learn what God requires of us in terms of our morality. Now, I could reference a dozen or more passages which deal with this issue. Instead, I will point out Jesus has very conveniently summarized it for us:

"'And you shall love the Lord your God with all your heart and with all your soul and with all your mind and with all your strength.' The second is this: 'You shall love your neighbor as yourself.' There is no other commandment greater than these" (Mark 12:30-31).

It does not matter who we are, where we are from, by what name we call ourselves, the label of our religion, or anything else about us: If we organize our lives based on the above quotation, we — like the scribe to whom Jesus was speaking — will not be far from the kingdom of God. In these two verses, Jesus reveals the key which unlocks the door to humanity's salvation.

One of the most important habits of the spiritually tough is to learn how to love God and our neighbors with an intentionality beyond all reason. We do this when we make this insane form of trust our operating principle; our *raison d'être*.

There is a wonderfully funny illustration of this concept from the movie *Bull Durham*.[8] In this cinematic fable, a rookie baseball pitcher by the name of 'Nuke' LaLoosch (played brilliantly by actor Tim Robbins) struggles on the pitcher's mound until he begins to do what his catcher (played equally brilliantly by Kevin Costner) tells him to do, "Don't think. Just throw what I tell you to throw." LaLoosch finally succeeds by trusting 'Crash' Davis. This movie demonstrates just how profoundly we can improve our lives when we begin to trust in a truth beyond our ability to control or even understand.

The game of baseball is — like so many sports — a metaphor of our faith-life inasmuch that when we step out onto the field of play willing to abide by a set of rules we did not create, we find the freedom to serve and achieve sometimes beyond our wildest hopes. God has created this field of play we call the world. Then he challenges all of us to love both him and our neighbors beyond all reason. These are the top rules in his rulebook. His promise to us is if we trust him, we will discover a range of freedom and success unlike any we have ever before experienced. But, you might ask, "How do I practice this love for God and my neighbors until it becomes habitual within me?"

One strategy is for us to pick out the person or group who — up to this point in our lives — has been our most-hated adversary. Ideally, I am talking about someone we could literally kill if given half a chance. Once we have this person or group in our minds, pause and recall how our hatred of them comes in large part because we have been thinking and acting using strength-language. This very same strength-language is what has been telling us we won't be satisfied until this person or group is eliminated.

Now consider them instead using the language and habits of the spiritually tough. Whatever harm they have done or are trying to inflict on us, we can deflected with the whole armor of God — especially with the shield of faith. In addition, we are able to meet the power of our enemy's worldly strength with the even more powerful truth of the gospel. At the heart of this gospel is Jesus' call for us to love radically. With the weapon of radical love, we can now see whatever strength they have will become irrelevant before the power of God's truth. We have just removed the lion's claws… the shark's teeth. We are able to overcome our enemy's hatred of us by our love of them. We may be bruised, battered, and bleeding but we will be able to stand on the last day because:

"The Lord is able to make him stand" (Romans 14:4).

Daring to irrationally love in this way — using standards God has created — is the clearest indication we are taking-on the habit of seeking after God's call-to-service. The reason this is so comes from the apostle John:

"If anyone says, 'I love God', and hates his brethren, he is a liar; for he who does not love… whom he has seen cannot love God whom he has not seen. And this commandment we have from him: whoever loves God must also love his brethren" (1 John 4:20-21).

Overcoming our quite rational hatred of our fellow human beings with irrational love is something so difficult I have made it the focus of Chapter 10. Too often, though, we never get to test whether we can love others in such a radical way because the worst enemy we would like to eliminate is the enemy within our own self.

Coveting God's call to service continues with an act of self-love.

How can a person love his neighbor or God if he can't even love himself? Before we begin to seek out what God wishes for us to do with the gifts of the Spirit with which he has blessed us, we must wrestle to the ground our self-hatred. If our desire for salvation is in any way genuine, then dealing with this deadly attitude is something we do after we stop doing that bone-headed thing we had been doing but before we begin to listen for God's call to service.

You got it! We are back at the step of removing our mind from that dark, smelly place it has been inhabiting for too long. Central to the process of getting real with our sins is the need to come face-to-face with our self-hatred. This means admitting we have been living inside an attitudinal latrine! We begin to banish this toxic mind-set only when we identify and understand what put us there in the first place: strength-language.

Perhaps we prefer to label the origin of this attitude as satanic.[9] However we see it, we feel self-hatred because things outside of us want us to be crippled by our past to the point where we can't imagine ever again being whole. But, this is not what God desires for us. What he says to us is this:

"If God is for us, who can be against us? He who did not spare his own Son but gave him up for us all, how will he not also with him graciously give us all things? Who shall bring any charge against God's elect? It is God who justifies. Who is to condemn? Christ Jesus is the one who died — more than that, who was raised — who is at the right hand of God, who indeed is interceding for us. Who shall separate us from the love of Christ? Shall tribulation, or distress, or persecution, or famine, or nakedness, or danger, or the sword?" (Romans 8:31-35)

Don't you find it interesting that the apostle Paul did *not* include self-hatred in his list of things which are unable to separate us from God's love? I believe it is absent for the simple reason our attitude of self-hatred is the enemy's *only* way of separating us from the love of God.

The world (or Satan) accomplishes this by getting us to do the separating when quite literally nothing else in all the universe can! For this reason, self-hatred is the most important attitude we need to purge from our minds as we come face-to-face with our sins.

But, how can we do this so long as we live, think, and act using the world's strength-language as the basis for our faith-life? Strength-language creates the conditions under which self-hatred becomes possible — and even necessary — for us to use in our spiritual journey. It does this by conning us into believing God hates us, personally, and not merely our sinfulness. And — so this poisonous thinking goes — if God hates us, why should we not also hate ourselves? Consequently, if we hate ourselves, does that not also make it easier for us to hate others? Finally, how much of the world's politics is fueled by someone's hatred of a person or group they imagine God also hates? Do such people believe this shared hatred makes them more acceptable in God's eyes? I am guessing they must.

The power which I have named spiritual toughness can shield us from self-hatred and all its consequences if we permit the truth of this new way of thinking to penetrate into and drive away our darkest thoughts. By doing this, we break the habit of trying and failing to draw closer to God through spiritual strength. This is because the spiritually tough person is able, eventually, to learn from his or her mistakes. That comes next.

5

Habit #4: Draw Lessons From the Past

One consequence of strength-language is the so-called weak person often remains crippled by past actions.

At the tail end of the previous chapter, I touched on the tendency for us to be hobbled by our mistakes. Now is a good time to expand on this subject in greater detail. I would like to begin doing so by speaking about a controversy involving the TV show *The Biggest Loser* which floated around the internet in January of 2015. If I am recalling this correctly, it seemed at least some past contestants complained of being brow-beaten by their trainers to their faces or through emails. According to season three contestant Kai Hibbard, the torment included statements like this: "It's because you are fat. Look at all the fat you have on you."[1]

I hope this isn't broadly descriptive of the attitudes of the persons in charge of this show, but I have to say, if it is, I would not be the least bit surprised. We are talking about fitness trainers, after all. Of course they speak the world's strength-language. Fitness trainers are among the top gurus promoting the success-through-strength mantra. It is their stock-in-trade.

Having said this, we should remember strength-language can occupy a necessary place in our lives. We must still contend with living in this world, after all. It's just that strength-language happens to be the worst guiding tenet to choose when it comes to organizing a faith-life. Yet most of us are daily taking these strength principles and blithely applying them to our walk with God. This is one of those big, fat, soul-crushingly stupid mistakes I freely admit to having made in my life. While I confess to being unfamiliar as to how these strength principles fare in other religions, I now know for certain — after almost thirty years in ministry — they are completely incompatible with Christianity. Christians have Jesus to thank for this.

It is easy for us to forget or ignore Jesus did the majority of the heavy lifting involved when it comes to our salvation. He did this by being unlawfully scourged, by dying on a cross, by descending to hell, and finally by being resurrected from the dead. God, through his Son, accomplished for us what was impossible for any human to do for his or her own self.

For many people, embracing this free gift of God's grace is too simple a thing to accept. It reminds me of the story of this powerful man who had a serious skin problem. When given what seemed to be a cure too simple for him, he complained:

"'Go and wash in the Jordan seven times, and your flesh shall be restored, and you shall be clean.' But Naaman was angry and went away, saying, 'Behold, I thought that he would surely come out to me and stand and call upon the name of the Lord his God, and wave his hand over the place and cure the leper'" (2 Kings 5:10-11).

Like Naaman, we imagine we must participate in some grand scheme so as to feel worthy enough to accept the prize of God's forgiveness. All this righteousness-through-good-works thinking disappears, however, when we are confronted with Jesus' "light yoke" admonition to:

"...believe also in me" (John 14:1).

Too many of us hear this simple solution to our problem of separation from God and think, "Surely God must require more from me!" So, we cast down the crown of victory given to us freely and begin our quest for a salvation through strength... or wealth... or influence... or anything which will grab God's attention to the amazing things we have achieved in his name with our lives.

Now, our tendency to do this is completely logical. The exceptional people among us do not achieve greatness by having it handed to them. Why should we believe it works any differently when it comes to our faith-life? But, earthly achievement and spiritual salvation are two very different goals sought after using two very different strategies, each of which must be thought about, discussed, and pursued using the appropriate language. These strategies and languages are neither interchangeable nor compatible.

Another problem with earthly achievement is there is always someone who manages to achieve more than we have. Once we begin to measure our achievements against the Warren Buffets, the Tom Bradys, or the Kate Uptons of this world, we can't help but to feel as if we have fallen short. Now, some of us use these feelings of inadequacy to spur us on to greater success. For folk like this the adage, "If at first I don't succeed, try, try again," is a driving principle.

In contrast to thousands of people who each occupy the top spot in their particular area of expertise are millions of others who do not and never will. And most of us are all right with the knowledge we will never be anything more than average. But a problem arises when we get to thinking God is just another of these things to which we can't measure up. We might begin to question why we should even care about faith in the first place if we come to the conclusion that — in our quest for salvation — our strivings are simply not enough to get us to where we want to be because that place is already occupied by someone else.

Strength-language wants us to believe all success — including faith in God —is a zero-sum game.[2] In this mind-set, faith in a savior like Jesus Christ becomes just one more contest with winners and losers; salvation is limited; and God's attention is widely dispersed. And because we haven't achieved anything of substance, this means God hasn't noticed us and therefore we won't be saved.

The sad consequence of this attitude is millions of people feeling themselves to be unworthy of God's love. This is one way to be crippled by our past mistakes. Adult Christians fall away from the faith of their youth because they believe themselves to be the biggest losers too weak for God to care about.

I have counseled people who are possessed of this belief. The irony is the people who have been feeding them the snake-oil theology responsible for this attitude often say it because they believe it about themselves and don't want to risk someone close to them achieving something they cannot. Misery sometimes demands company.

This attitude is held and spread by millions of people who have been conned or convinced into believing faith in God is forged the same way and using the same human strength it takes to achieve any great and lasting success in this world. Naturally, anyone who isn't able to do this is labelled a "loser." Only when we reorganize our thinking and acting around the idea of being spiritually tough can we free ourselves from this mental shackle and begin to learn from our mistakes.

In the area of our faith-life, this means understanding salvation is a gift available to everyone in the world and not something we earn. Second, it means when we continue to allow past sins to stymie our current desire for a relationship with God, this is evidence we are still thinking, speaking, and acting using strength-language. If so, we must turn away from this mind-set knowing we are only weak and a loser so long as we continue to think the way the world, or Satan, wants us to think.

Our failings can be our best teachers, but first we must acknowledge the truth.

"So Jesus said to the Jews who had believed in him, 'If you abide in my word, you are truly my disciples, and you will know the truth, and the truth will set you free.' They answered him, 'We are offspring of Abraham and have never been enslaved to anyone. How is it that you say, "You will become free?"' Jesus answered them, 'Truly, truly, I say to you, everyone who commits sin is a slave to sin'" (John 8:31-34).

When we were thinking, acting, and speaking using the language of spiritual strength, we were terrified of failure. If we did some bone-headed thing, we just about died to think how inadequate we were before God. So, we hid our sins from him just like Adam and Eve did. We also hid them from our parents, our children, our spouses, and our government. Worst of all, we hid them from ourselves lest we remembered our sins and realized just how weak and enslaved we really were.

I remember how much energy this strategy took and the depth of my spiritual exhaustion when I thought this way about my faith. I remember the stress of trying to maintain the persona of someone who was *with it* all the while knowing inside myself I wasn't really that strong person. I also remember that scene from the movie *Ghostbusters* where a city electrician shuts off the power grid holding back entities locked away in a psycho-kinetic vault. When the force-field is shut down, all hell breaks loose upon the unsuspecting people of New York City.[3] Of course — in confronting our failings — we fear happening to us what befell the terrified New Yorkers in that movie. Now, our doing this is not nearly as funny as that scene, but it is just as painful. Thank goodness it is, because pain is an excellent teacher of important truths.

As uncomfortable as facing the pain of our sin can be, it is even worse to bottle up this pain behind a wall of emotional strength. Anyone who has had to face PTSD issues or who counsels someone with this disorder will say it is a far better thing to bring trauma out into the open where the light of day can sanitize these demons.[4] Besides which, we just aren't strong enough to hold back all our sins and failings. Eventually, the pain will crush us if we don't get out from underneath it. Also, as long as we keep our sins locked away in a mental vault, we are denied the chance of learning from them. Admitting we can never be strong enough and that acknowledging our sins is a good thing are the twin truths which will set us free.

Chances are you are guilty of many a screw-up. Lord knows I am! Only we and God know what those sins are, but no matter what bone-headed things we have done, we have already experienced the pain of that moment. When we were acting on the basis of strength-language, our usual way of dealing with our failings was to forget about them and hope the person we hurt would eventually do the same or at least forgive us.

If only we could face our failures with the same tough enthusiasm Elon Musk brings to bear on his! If we did, we would at least derive some benefit from them instead of attempting to forget about the pain and humiliation, and failing to do even that.

Early in 2015, one of Mr. Musk's companies, SpaceX, sought to land the first stage of one of their Falcon 9 rockets on an unmanned barge off Florida's Atlantic coast. No one had ever contemplated doing this let alone actually tried it. In January, and again in April of that year, SpaceX failed in these attempts both spectacularly and publicly. And while obviously not pleased with the results, Mr. Musk's Twitter comments in the aftermath of both attempts reveal a man who understands failure to be a necessary component to any future success.[5]

His engineers learned quite a bit about the craft's guidance software, and the performance capabilities of the hypersonic grid fins built to control attitude, pitch, and yaw. After the first attempt, they learned they needed more hydraulic fluid. The second attempt taught them the consequences of a too-slow-to-respond valve. One day soon, Musk and SpaceX will get it right. Then he will get it right some of the time. Finally, those first stages will nail their orbital dismounts nearly every time. This will happen because one of the most important abilities of tough-minded people is their habit not just to acknowledge their mistakes, but to learn from them.

This habit is critically important for us in our faith-lives. Like the ability to embrace change, it is something we were born into this world to do. Additionally, it is a habit we acquire first and foremost for the benefit of others. By signaling we are willing to learn from our failings, we announce a shift away from selfishness and toward concern for the welfare of those around us.

When we were operating using strength-language, our desire to hide our sins and failings was all about us not looking weak to those closest to us. As Q once told cinematic strongman James Bond, "Never let them see you bleed."[6] The spiritually tough person, however, understands how God uses us — as beaten and bloodied as we might be — and how a large part of this use will be aimed at helping those around us. Like this:

"Brothers, if anyone is caught in any transgression, you who are spiritual should restore him in a spirit of gentleness. Keep watch on yourself, lest you too be tempted. Bear one another's burdens, and so fulfill the law of Christ" (Galatians 6:1-2).

Jesus, according to the apostle Paul, is the ultimate burden-bearer, and accomplishes this by his ability to overcome all worldly power thrown at him up to and including capital punishment. This is the "law of Christ" referred to above. It does not mean we are to seek after martyrdom as if the law of Christ was about us becoming as strong as our Lord. Rather, we are to remind ourselves whatever sins have been committed against us or by us, Christ has already borne away to hell and back again. For the Christian, what this law does require is his or her life to be lived in grateful acknowledgement of Jesus' sacrifice.

If we are able to think on this truth, then we are in a place of spiritual toughness where we can focus on a transgressor's or our own restoration instead of the pain we feel from having sinned or been sinned against. If we can accept the truth which testifies Jesus Christ already has done the heavy lifting required for us to attain the kingdom of God, then the ability to learn from our failings is within our reach. Our faith-life has now transitioned over to how best we can help someone else bear the burden of their failings and sins. The example of our spiritual toughness gleaned from genuinely facing our sin and pain is something we can impart.

Spiritually tough people are able to transform their failings into positive actions.

Unlike the fictional Mr. Bond, we should allow our family, friends, and neighbors to see us bruised, battered, and bleeding from the world's attempt to do us in. Even more, we should permit those same people the honor of taking front row seats as we claim our pain and demonstrate what we have learned from the experience. We should do this even if they are still operating under the influences of strength-language. We should do this without regard to their faith-life journey. We should do it because we are now drawing lessons from our past instead of being crippled by that past.

Whereas spiritual strength was about not looking like a loser (hence all the hiding of our true selves), spiritual toughness is about accepting our failings and transforming them into positive actions. Here is an example of what I'm talking about:

"So Joseph said to his brothers, 'Come near to me, please.' And they came near. And he said, 'I am your brother Joseph, whom you sold into Egypt. And now do not be dismayed or angry with yourselves because you sold me here, for God sent me before you to preserve life'" (Genesis 45:4-5).

The Joseph Cycle — as biblical scholars call the book of Genesis from Chapters 37 to 47 — is one of the most important stories in all of Scripture.[7] I encourage you to open a Bible and read it. It is a grand story of redemption — not just concerning Joseph's brothers who are guilty of murdering their brother in their hearts, but also about Joseph's own transformation from an arrogant upstart to someone God could use to preserve life.

Everyone in this story is forced to come face-to-face with his failings. First, it is Joseph's and then his brothers' turn. Consequently, instead of Joseph using the sins committed against him as a pretext for retaliation, he reaches down into the furnace of spiritual toughness to forge something positive: reconciliation and love.

Remember, Jesus has already preserved our lives through the loving reconciliation of the cross and the empty tomb. And he did this act of grace so you and I might be free to forge our own positive actions in the lives of the people to which we are most closely connected.

The world saw in June of 2015 a contemporary version of this story play out in the bucolic streets of Charleston, South Carolina. Nine members of a historically black church in that city were murdered while in the midst of a Bible Study lesson. Like acts of terrorism elsewhere in the world, the killer imagined his actions would spark more hatred and retaliatory attacks. Instead, he was publicly forgiven by the families of his victims.[8] Instead of more violence, love and unity blossomed. Grace vanquished brutish ignorance. Worldly strength was overcome by spiritual toughness.

Each of us — like Joseph, his brothers, and the people of Charleston, South Carolina — has a past which is filled with drama if not trauma. Ignoring it or trying to conceal it under a mask of strength is a dead-end strategy. But if we have been using strength-language to speak about our faith, that is exactly what we have been doing. Instead — like the people from the stories I have shared here — let us learn something valuable from our mistakes and the tragedies which have come into our lives.

Let us be spiritually tough and permit the truth of God's mercy to forge in us a future filled with love and reconciliation. Not only may we melt someone else's icy heart as they take note of our transformed lives, this change in us may also blow apart the structure of entitlement we have built up around our faith-life. Now, hold onto your hat; the next habit of the spiritually tough is all about becoming more grateful.

6

Habit #5: Feel Gratitude Instead of Entitlement

Human attitudes concerning entitlement run deep and have done so for a long time.

"**And Jesus said to his disciples, 'Truly, I say to you, only with difficulty will a rich person enter the kingdom of heaven.' When the disciples heard this, they were greatly astonished, saying, 'Who then can be saved?' But Jesus looked at them and said, 'With man this is impossible, but with God all things are possible.' Then Peter said in reply, 'See, we have left everything and followed you. What then will we have?'**" (Matthew 19:23, 25-27)

Peter's question, "What then will we have?" has been repeated over and over again by millions of people in the nearly two thousand years since he first asked it. And it will likely ever be asked as long as there are people in the world. The apostle expresses for all of us — albeit concerning his place in heaven — the single, most important concern we have as human beings: How will we get what we need to have in order to live?

And it is not as if we are greedy creatures; most of us just want the basics. Give us three square meals a day, a roof over our heads, some dignified work for our hands, a measure of security for our family, and the choice to believe in God or not as we see fit. Do we have that? Great! Now, leave us be. We will figure the rest out for ourselves.

But, what are we to do when we find ourselves seemingly surrounded by successful people while we feel like the only ones not invited to the party? Who among us wouldn't be insulted? What person among us wouldn't seek after some kind of redress of their grievances? Who am I kidding? We all would!

If University of Maryland student blogger Brianna Patterson is correct, most young adults have, until recently, cared too much for the high octane lifestyles of the rich and famous. It is her contention America's obsessive fixation about the glamorous among us is being replaced by a "surge" of entertainment shows which celebrate the lives of ordinary people.[1] Is this trend evidence of an America no longer content to obsess on the rise and fall of elites? Have we, instead, decided to extend world-wide invitations to our own parties? Perhaps, but it is also possible this is just one more example of artist Andy Warhol's famous prediction coming to pass about everyone, at some point, getting his or her "fifteen minutes of fame."

It seems to me there are two powerful illusions at play here. The first is the rich and famous have it together when it is very clear not all of them do. The second is ordinary people can't forge success when it is very clear many can. I believe all we want — no matter who we are — is to be told the rules of the game and then be left alone to succeed or fail by the sweat of our own brow. That we are no longer afforded the dignity of doing this in private due to the intrusion of technology is something most of us grudgingly accept and a few of us choose to exploit.

There is a problem, however, when we come to believe those rules have been stacked against us. And it is important to understand this is something which can happen at every level of our society. Nobody wants to participate in any kind of rigged contest, but especially not when the lives and health of our families are on the line. Yet, this is precisely the situation American sociologist Lester Ward identified over one hundred years ago. Below is his voice as preserved by historian Henry Steel Commager in his comprehensive work entitled, "The American Mind: An Interpretation of American Thought and Character Since the 1880s":

"Nothing is more obvious today than the signal inability of capital and private enterprise to take care of themselves unaided by the state; and while they are incessantly denouncing "paternalism," by which they mean the claim of the defenseless laborer and artisan to a share in this lavish state protection, they are all the while besieging legislatures for relief from their own incompetency, and "pleading the baby act" through a trained body of lawyers and lobbyists" (Lester F. Ward, Forum XX, 1895).[2]

This Gilded Age observation at first blush seems like something drawn from the pages of a recent *New York Times* Op Ed or a missive tossed like a Molotov cocktail into the midst of last week's political sniping on *Meet the Press*. Unfortunately, Ward never paneled a Sunday morning TV round-table discussion. Instead, he was a solitary, but vocal critic — through the medium of print — of what was in his day called *laissez-faire* economics.[3]

Practitioners of this philosophy still exist today, and they are still of the mind-set which believes — in all things human-related — only the financially strong should survive. Commager also affirmed Ward's observation that the great agents of American capitalism often acquired their assets through the benefit of government intervention or legislation, and that, "only artificial competition remained, and it operated best in a framework of minimum interference."[4] Today, this same idea is expressed in a concept called "corporate welfare."

For both Commager and Ward, one antidote to corporate welfare was to be found in those social-liberal leanings which eventually came into full flower under Franklin Roosevelt's New Deal programs. Having the national government "remake society along happier lines" corrected the imbalance caused by the corrupted *laissez-faire* economics of the Robber Barons.[5]

So, it is no accident we live in a society dominated by a pervasive welfare-state mentality. From the people living in the swankiest penthouses to the homeless person on the street below and everyone in between, there is embedded in our culture (and in our government) the sense we are entitled to something. Often, we are not even able to name precisely what this *something* is, but this attitude sticks to us like the humidity of a Midwestern summer's day.

By now, it should come as no surprise to read I believe entitlement's origins are from strength-language. The attitude of entitlement is created from the chasm which exists between the ideals of success to which we aspire and the degree of that success in our lives. In a world of gross injustice, entitlement becomes — for "winners" — a means of staying at the top. For those who perceive themselves to be "losers," entitlement is their way of staying alive.

Tweak the tax code to favor the big oil companies; offer everyone two years of free college education; seek assistance from your local food pantry; ask a city council for a tax abatement: these are all examples of things which can feed our belief we should be seeking after and getting something we are owed. Like puppies before their mother, we want what we want when we want it and entitlement is the way of achieving this goal. End of story.

And it really would be the end of the story if it were not for the fact at least some of us desire a life with God. Now, that is a good thing except we are born into a welfare state-of-mind world. We breathe its air, we eat its food, and we wash in the magic waters of its philosophical rivers. How could we not but apply these ideas of entitlement to our quest for heaven?

Can we be blamed for thinking we are also entitled to eternal life? Uh, yeah, we can. Because, the truth about our salvation has always been readily accessible to us and it does not involve entitlement. Sorry to say, but we are not and have never been entitled to a seat at the great banquet table in heaven. That ticket gets punched by *sola fide*: faith alone.[6] Those who believe they will be welcomed into heavenly glory with open arms by virtue of how much they have been expecting this glory are going to be in for a major shock.

The spiritually tough person, on the other hand, employs a different set of principles as he or she navigates through this welfare state-of-mind world in which we must live. We will get to gratitude in a moment. First, though, I want to speak about our need to habituate acceptance.

We must trade-in our expectations for acceptance.

Most of us live life with peace making infrequent visits to our neighborhood. Much of this lack of calm is of the world's making. Some of it we have to take responsibility for. Either way, please also allow me to share with you what I've told many other people: A lack of peace in our lives is largely about having unmet expectations. If we aren't at peace, this is God giving us an opportunity to jettison our expectations.

Better yet, trade in those expectations and the feelings of entitlement which give birth to them. Trade them in for an attitude of acceptance. That is because acceptance is a vital habit of the spiritually tough. Damn, but if this isn't also one of the hardest things for me to do!

As my wife would be only too happy to confirm, I hate to lose at cards. But, what I hate even more is a game which gets wildly out of control to the point where all sense of competition goes right out the window. I have been known to cheat myself out of some advantage in order to level the competition and make the game more fun. (She can't stand this, in case your were wondering.)

In this, I am just like Alice from the "Alice in Wonderland" stories who gives herself great advice, but very rarely follows it. That advice, of course, is: "Jordy, just play the cards as they are dealt." But acceptance is not an easy attitude for me to habituate. I'm probably not alone in this. For me, it is because acceptance works against my innate sense of justice.

A well-developed sense of justice is what lays behind the indignity of getting stopped for driving three miles-per-hour over the speed limit when not more than five minutes earlier, somebody sped past you going at least ten miles-per-hour faster. It is what prompts one kid to come to the defense of another kid getting bullied on the school playground. Justice is what tells us we have the right to expect the price of food to be stable in times of crisis, our children to be safe in their classrooms, and our utilities and roads to be restored in a timely manner after a natural disaster. It is good to have ideals and justice is one of the best as far as that goes. But when someone like me says, "Accept the world as it is," we feel like we can't unless we abandon our desire for justice.

Well, I am here to say we don't have to do without justice in our lives. However, I do urge us to relocate this ideal to where it will be the most effective: in God's capable hands. If we can do this, it will be easier for us to welcome acceptance into our lives.

Acceptance is like looking out the window (as I am doing now) and observing that the church parking lot cleared of snow yesterday needs to be cleared again today. Unlike having expectations which often pertain to the world the way we want it to be, adopting an attitude of acceptance is about meeting the world the way it is.[7]

This attitude is not the same as feeling resignation. Resignation is a kind of defeat we experience when our expectations are dashed. Acceptance, on the other hand, is the mental state of harboring few, if any, expectations to begin with. Here is a story from the Bible about a woman who understood the differences between the two:

"And behold, a Canaanite woman from that region came out and was crying, 'Have mercy on me, O Lord, Son of David; my daughter is severely oppressed by a demon.' But he did not answer her a word. And his disciples came and begged him, saying, 'Send her away, for she is crying out after us.' He answered, 'I was sent only to the lost sheep of the house of Israel.' But she came and knelt before him, saying, 'Lord, help me.' And he answered, 'It is not right to take the children's bread and throw it to the dogs.' She said, 'Yes, Lord, yet even the dogs eat the crumbs that fall from their masters' table'" (Matthew 15:22-27).

This non-Jewish woman effects the restoration of her daughter because she accepts rather than expects Jesus to perform this miracle. Jesus tells this unnamed woman her faith is great, and certainly compared to the Jewish leadership who were actively seeking to kill him, her faith was.

Here is a list of the things the Canaanite woman accepted: first she accepted Jesus as the Messiah (this is evidenced by her referring to him as "Son of David"); then she accepted she must abase herself; next, she accepted Jesus' description of her as a dog. (Ouch!) Lastly, the woman was willing to accept whatever crumbs of grace Jesus might sprinkle down upon her, for she is confident enough (or desperate enough) to trust it will be sufficient to free her daughter from demonic oppression.

I say this woman got what she needed for her daughter because she was one tough yet humble pagan! Like Jesus' similar encounter with a centurion, we have to wonder if she didn't leave the Lord asking why the people he came to save didn't have even a fraction of her attitude of gratitude. Well, maybe that's the exact problem: It is difficult to be grateful with a head full of expectation and a belly full of entitlement. The Jews of Jesus' day wanted the messiah they expected instead of accepting the one God sent them. Not so the Canaanite woman! Too many Christians today have the same problem the Jewish people of old had. But, gratitude concerning what Jesus Christ did for us becomes a whole lot easier after we trade away our expectations for acceptance.

Spiritually tough people model gratitude.

If we wake up each day and are able to list no more than ten things for which we are grateful, chances are we still have a head filled with expectations. Expectations seem like wonderful things to have. Our children are full of them just before Christmas or their birthdays. We too feel expectation when our team is playing in the World Cup, the Super Bowl, the World Series, etc. Expectation, though, has a tendency to rob us of joy. After all, if we expect to get great gifts or our team to win the big game — and then that very thing happens — all life has done is to have met our expectations. There is no opportunity for having those expectations surpassed. Alternately, if our expectations are not met, we feel let-down. In my way of thinking, it is a far better strategy for us to model gratitude because unlike expectation, gratitude always leads us to joy.

Modeling gratitude is the natural outgrowth of habituating acceptance. On the surface, this may sound like a strategy of lowering our expectations. It's not. Playing the expectations game in any form (high or low) continues to draw us away from spiritual toughness back toward spiritual strength because expectations are forms of control. Acceptance and its partner gratitude, however, are more compatible with the strategy of managing our lives.

One of the consequences of adopting the habits of the spiritually tough is the emergence of something I call "spiritual synergy."[8] All habits of the spiritually tough are synergistic in that when we partner habit with habit, the effect is multiplicative rather than merely additive.

The ability to embrace change coupled with seeking God's call combined with gratitude has the power to open our minds to even deeper and richer understandings of what our place is in the world. This spiritual synergy would be like giving our eyes the ability to see light far beyond the visible spectrum humans are limited to seeing. Imagine that!

But trying to model gratitude while still having a head filled with expectation is a lot like trying to run with thirty-pound weights around our ankles: it is possible to do it, but why would we want to? So, undo those anchors, unshackle your faith-life from expectation, and win your freedom from entitlement. If we can do this, we will find it easier to count our blessings. This phrase is not just a line from a Bing Crosby song; I mean it in a literal sense.

Count them all! Each of us should make a list and not let ourselves stop at one hundred or even two hundred items. Now, post them where we will see them: on our fridge; in our car; next to our bathroom mirror; in our office. Let us give our sense of gratitude a solid foundation. Put that list where our friends and family can see it. (We are modeling gratitude, here, not just feeling grateful.) Finally, we should pray.

I have no idea if you are a person of faith in God or not. And in terms of the habits of the spiritually tough, the object of your devotion may not matter all that much at this point. You may even be an atheist. So what? Pray anyway. I'm not saying for you necessarily to pray to God. All I am saying is prayer is one of the most important ways of modeling gratitude. Prayer takes us out of the emotional muck which is our mind and challenges us to think on someone or something greater than ourselves.[9]

Praying reminds us that whatever we have in this world, we sure as heck didn't get it by ourselves! In fact, unless you (by some miracle) gave birth to yourself, you can take credit for nothing in your life including your life. From the moment our lungs drew in that first breath, every good and lasting thing which has come to us has been a gift.

Modeling gratitude begins with becoming aware.

It is difficult to be grateful with our awareness turned off. Over lunch one day, find an outdoor cafe and just sit there with your meal and observe people. I guarantee you will witness countless acts of generosity — along with a smattering of brutish behavior. But the challenge here is to look for a few of the ARK's — Acts (of) Random Kindness — people commit by the thousands every day. When I did this, I was amazed at what I saw. You, too, should be amazed at what your senses detect.

Here is another exercise: commit yourself to paying special attention to what your closest family members and friends are doing for you. Then make opportunities to thank them no fewer than a dozen times every day. Tell them you are learning how to model gratitude and would appreciate their help by not cringing every time they hear you expressing that thanks.

While doing this, we must continue to flush away our recurrent feelings of entitlement and the expectations which generate them. To this end, we also should make a list of these things and cross them off again and again when they rear their ugly heads. Eventually, those old, useless weights on our faith-life will get the memo and go disappear back into the realm of strength-language.

Finally let us remember gratitude goes hand-in-hand with acceptance. We must be willing to accept the world as it presents itself to us; the bad along with the good. If some tragedy thrusts itself into our lives, pause for a moment, take a deep breath or two, pray and then make a list of things for which we are grateful instead of focusing on our pain. We might be surprised just how much this one technique can lower our anxieties during a time of crisis.[10]

Modeling gratitude is evidence we have habituated acceptance. Our gratitude then can act as a shield against the power from the world. The more we remain grateful and model gratitude, the more we are able to withstand the "slings and arrows of outrageous fortune," as William Shakespeare put it. Remember, the goal is to become spiritually tough because toughness will almost always outlasts strength. Then there is that other important consequence: joy.

Experiencing a joy-filled life is not a prerequisite or in any way a requirement on our journey to God's kingdom. But, it sure is a nice bonus! Our living with fewer expectations opens up opportunities for being surprised by the ARK's others shower down around us. Habituating acceptance enhances our ability to notice them. Modeling gratitude insures we acknowledge the sources of our joy be they temporal or divine. And all this is important because the next habit of the spiritually tough is arguably the most challenging one of all: The spiritually tough are in the habit of risking everything.

7

Habit #6: Risk it All

Fear of failure is an illusion created and sustained by strength-language.

Most of us have seen the movie *Indiana Jones and the Last Crusade*. During the movie's climatic scene, Professor Henry Jones, Jr. must face three challenges before he is able to retrieve the Holy Grail in order to save his wounded and dying father. The third test of faith is a leap from the lion's head. We see Harrison Ford's character take a deep breath, compose himself, center his mind on what he really believes about Christianity, lift his foot, and....

....discover that what looks to him to be a step out onto nothing is merely an illusion. A solid stone bridge was there all the time. Phew! What a relief for both him and the audience to find out faith in God is just a matter of optics.[1]

You might think that as a pastor and theologian I would be of the opinion director Stephen Spielberg erred in presenting the idea of a leap of faith in this manner. That judgment might indeed be expected of someone like myself, but in my case it would also be wrong. In my opinion, Mr.

Spielberg nailed it. Faith in God is and always has been, first and foremost, a matter of how we perceive the world around us.

Do you want to know something really obnoxious? So is fear. This is especially true when it comes to fear of failure. Fear of failure is one of the chief illusions which can be and too often is an obstacle blocking our faith journey. But, fear of failure is a mirage in no small part because it comes out of the world's strength-language; something which I contend to be a bankrupt paradigm.

If we organize our thinking and doing around strength-language, then our lives become all about winning or losing. Take a moment right now to assess how much you judge your life using this metric. When I did this for myself, I was horrified by what I discovered.

How we frame the meaning of our lives matters. As I said awhile back, if we see our existence as just one facet of an immense zero-sum game, the probability of failure looms so large in our psyche that the fear of failure seems impossible to avoid.

If it has been awhile since you've read 1 Samuel 28, I urge you to pause reading this book and go look it up. Read it and come right back. But before you do, here is a snippet to whet your whistle:

"So Saul disguised himself and put on other garments and went, he and two men with him. And they came to the woman by night. And he said, 'Divine for me a spirit and bring up for me whomever I shall name you.' Then the woman said, 'Whom shall I bring up for you?' He said, 'Bring up Samuel for me'" (1 Samuel 28:8, 11).

All done? Well, you just read one of the best character studies on fear of failure ever composed. As you may or may not know, the Bible is not just the revealed word of God, it also contains some of the best literature ever written.[2]

Saul's encounter with the necromancer — this female medium in En-dor — exemplifies the desperate lengths people sometimes will go to in order to keep from failing. But no amount of cheating, no amount of relying on his own strength could make up for Saul's egregious lack of faith in God. Soon after this sad seance, Saul pays for this mistake with his life. Saul's fate was set the moment he decided it was better to rely on his own strength than on God's. Like many of us are prone to doing, Saul didn't just walk on the road of faithlessness, he ran headlong down it.

Awhile back, I wrote about how we all live in a welfare state-of-mind world. Anyone who seeks after some advantage outside the rules of whatever system they are part of is, by definition, infected with this mentality. Besides being filled with entitlement, such a person may be so afraid to fail that they look for ways to game the system. Unfortunately, such a person will fail because failure is inevitable once he or she decides to operate by the habits of strength instead of by the habits of toughness. That light at the end of the tunnel... for the person afraid to fail, it is not their liberation at hand, but a train bearing down on them. Or, as Jesus said to his disciples on the occasion of his arrest in the Garden of Gethsemane:

"'Put your sword back in its place. For all who take [up] the sword will perish by the sword'" (Matthew 26:52b) [bracketed word is mine].

Fear of failure is one of the most powerful brakes on our actions.

An even worse outcome can occur when the person who fears failure finds himself or herself frozen into inaction. Think back to the image of King Saul prone on the ground; bereft of strength and bathed in fear like he was undoubtedly bathed in his own bodily fluids. Fear of failure can keep us from making decisions — both good ones and poor ones. Who among us hasn't ever thought this: "It is better to just let it happen. That way, I might be able to shift blame away from me. But, if I try and don't succeed, the fault is all mine."

Think of all the things in our lives which have not been accomplished because we were frozen in place by fear of failure. I hope your list is short. Mine isn't. Regardless of its size, break out the kitchen timer, again… and set it for five minutes, again. After it goes off, know that the truth has set you free from all these regrets. Fear and failure are concepts linked to the habits of people who succumb to the illusion that strength matters. You and I are no longer that kind of person.

Those who practice the habits of spiritual toughness see a different reality. To employ another movie metaphor, this is the spiritual toughness equivalent of the kid from the first *Matrix* movie who says to Neo, "There is no spoon."[3] This kid knew something which Neo didn't: fear and failure, like faith, are about our reality not being what it *appears* to be.

Our perspective on the world changes everything about our relationship to the world. So, when we turn our thinking and speaking and especially our doing away from strength to toughness, we eliminate fear of failure altogether because failure itself is no longer relevant. How could it be? Almighty God, through the Messiah, has "gamed" the system for us; if we have faith.

Fear of success is just as bad.

There is yet one more fear with which to contend. For some of us, it may seem like something impossible to experience. I am speaking here about fear of success. Not to be confused with performance anxiety (also known as stage fright), fear of success is often experienced by people who have been traumatized. The thrill from any possible success and the anxiety from the traumatic event become difficult to separate. So, they learn that if they avoid success, they also avoid reliving difficult moments in their lives.[4]

Fear of success may also be triggered in people who feel they have risen to a position beyond where the Peter Principle says they should be.

To remind us all, the Peter Principle posits the following: a person "rises to the highest level of their incompetence."[5] This axiom suggests success and failure are outcomes determined by an irrational marketplace, and that most of us eventually find ourselves in jobs for which we are supremely ill-suited.

It has taken me the better part of three decades to figure out why this axiom has rubbed me the wrong way. Now I know: everywhere I look, I see the Peter Principle being upheld! Our national politics alone is filled with men and women who are certainly ill-suited for success in that arena. By constantly lowering their own expectations about what they can accomplish politically, many politicians pretty much eliminate any fear which might arise from the pressure of having to do their jobs well.

Thankfully, for the person operating by spiritual toughness, the Peter Principle is moot. Nonetheless, fear of success is a real problem and one of the most difficult ideas for us to dislodge from our minds. But, when we do our thinking and deciding using the language of spiritual toughness, it is like pulling out by the taproot this weed of an idea. Or, if you prefer, think of success and failure as occupying two sides of the same coin. To transact using the currency of fear is to lose all hope of having a faith-life just as surely as King Saul lost his life on the gentle slopes of Mount Gilboa.

The world provides no safety net. In fact, the opposite is more the case.

"It is a dog eat dog world," so the saying goes. If we watch enough of the evening news, what we see will convince us it is and that we have no choice but to accept this condition. You might even remind me that I said, "The world is what it is and it cannot be changed." Perhaps both of us should consider this biblical quote:

"Do not love the world or the things of the world. If anyone loves the world, the love of the Father is not in him. For all that is in the world — the desires of the flesh and the desires of the eyes and pride in possessions — is not from the Father but is from the world. And the world is passing away along with its desires, but whoever does the will of God abides forever" (1 John 2:15-17).

We who go by the name Christian are supposed to be in the world while not being of the world.[6] I have heard it said we are tourists whose task is to transform the world as we take in the sights. A better analogy might be to compare us to people who volunteer to go into an area after a natural or man-made disaster. Christians without a clear sense of identity may find the sixth habit of spiritual toughness difficult to embrace. After all, nobody goes on a camera-ready holiday expecting then to roll up their sleeves and move rubble while looking for survivors.

Well, if we consider ourselves to be Christians yet are adamant about living our faith-life using strength-language, then we haven't read the memo. In fact, we have not only accepted the dog-eat-dog nature of our citizenship, but have chosen to remain blind to the sufferings of our fellow citizens. Some people do this and justify their actions by saying they have brought peace and beauty to their corner of creation. My answer is to say, "Great, but do not stop with yourself. Otherwise it is all about what you selfishly want." As the apostle John reminded us, the desires of the human heart are incompatible with the desire for a faith-life in God.

My point is this: the world indeed may be the way it is, but this is — as they say in the realm of debate — a straw-man argument.[7] Who cares that it is a dog-eat-dog world? The goal has never been for people of faith to make a home in this world, but to change the world through their relationship with God and each other. This only happens if we are able to — as the apostle Paul did with the scales over his eyes — slough-off strength-language in exchange for the new optics of spiritual toughness.

Just as anyone gambling in Las Vegas should expect to lose his or her shirt, so too should anyone attempting to win heaven using strength-language expect to come up short... and the world will not shed one tear for him or help her get back on her feet. The world and all its attractions is set up to kill us, and it has succeeded in doing just that in every case save one.

God does provide a safety net, and this allows us to risk it all.

"And if I go and prepare a place for you, I will come again and will take you to myself, that where I am you may be also. And you know the way to where I am going. Thomas said to him, 'Lord, we do not know where you are going. How can we know the way?' Jesus said to him, 'I am the way, the truth, and the life. No one comes to the Father except through me'" (John 14:3-6).

Jesus overcame the world by making irrelevant our search for strength apart from God. He did this not by strong-arming the world but by absorbing every stripe, every insult, and every sin the world (and we) could heap upon his bruised and bleeding body. Finally, he overcame death itself. This is what makes Jesus of Nazareth the exception to the rule about the world's success at killing us, and, likewise, what makes him the toughest person ever to walk this planet.

While Jesus was on excursion here, he left anyone who wanted one a pathway back to God. He thereby became the only safety net we will ever need or want. In fact, according to the witness of the apostle John quoted above, he is the only one there is.

The practical effect of this truth is realized in our new-found ability to focus on the habits of spiritual toughness rather than continuing in the misguided quest for the things strength-language says are important. To this end, the sixth habit in this new paradigm is the action of risking everything for the sake of sharing the good news which says we can, through faith, abide with the One, Eternal Mind of the universe. What would such risk-taking look like, or how would this new attitude be revealed in the daily choices which shape our character?

It probably would look like the daily choices a religious missionary makes in his or her life on the cutting edge of faith-sharing. As I write these words, a Presbyterian colleague and her family are in the final stages of returning from a two-year turn as missionaries to a Christian community in Cairo, Egypt. At times, they have been mere blocks from anti-Christian violence. And yet, this family's love for the community they travelled a third of the way around the world to serve never wavered.

Our presbytery officials asked the churches within its boundary to not share details either in print or online about this family's missionary work when these local churches wrote about it in their newsletters or church website blogs. There was concern Islamic militants in Cairo would be scanning such social media sites for clues as to the names and locations of these missionaries and others like them.

Unless we in our faith-lives are faced with choices of this magnitude and mortality, I would suggest we are not yet risking very much for the sake of the gospel of Jesus Christ. But, it is not as if this is merely some opinion I have plucked out of thin air:

"Whoever loves father or mother more than me is not worthy of me, and whoever loves son or daughter more than me is not worthy of me. And whoever does not take up his cross and follow me is not worthy of me. Whoever finds his life will lose it, and whoever loses his life for my sake will find it" (Matthew 10:37-39).

Jesus, in this passage, sets high the bar for discipleship. And just in case any of us is wondering; the "cross" to which he was referring is a metaphorical one. Not that it much matters; it is possible for a metaphorical cross to be as painful as if not more painful than the one he himself endured for our sakes.

Nothing speaks to our attraction to the world better than our bonds of familial love. Jesus, though, says we are to weigh our love of family against our love of him, and that our Christian discipleship only happens when we choose him over everything else in this life we hold dear. This is why I said risking everything is the most challenging habit among my list of ten.

Our only hope of meeting this challenge happens when we embrace a change in how we view the world around us. This perspective is shaped overwhelmingly by language because language is the primary medium of comprehension between the world and our brains. Language is how we put meaning to what our senses reveal to us every day. If this understanding is dominated by strength-language, we will value what our senses reveal more than what those senses cannot detect. The anonymous writer of Hebrews is far more eloquent than I in expressing this concept:

"Now faith is the assurance of things hoped for, the conviction of things not seen. For by it the people of old received their commendation. By faith we understand that the universe was created by the word of God, so that what is seen was not made out of things that are visible" (Hebrews 11:1-3).

If we love those whom we see more than we love Jesus whom we cannot see, then this is evidence we are living by sight and not by faith, and that we are full-fledged citizens of the world. We can claim all we want about having a relationship with Christ, but if we are living by sight, we are not, in fact, crisis interventionists out to change the faith-perspective of the natives. Our hesitation to risk only a few things let alone everything marks us as native occupants of this world.

I have struggled trying to implement this particular habit of spiritual toughness. Like many of us, I still live too much by sight and not enough by faith. The love for my family is difficult to set behind my love for Jesus. And yet this is precisely what I have been trying to do.

I have imagined myself in a situation where I am forced to renounce my allegiance to Christ or face watching one of my children being murdered in front of me. For folk like me living in America, this may be just an academic exercise. But for people of faith all across this globe, this horror is an every day reality. I ask myself how I would handle such a moment. As difficult as it would be to experience the loss of a child, I would not renounce the source of my eternal life.

When we engage in this or some similar mental exercise, we may yet find it easier to incorporate this risk-taking habit of spiritual toughness into our discipleship. The key to habituating this ability is found when we change the language by which we connect our brains to the world: we must adopt the perspective of spiritual toughness so we can see the world and our place in it as it truly is and not as it merely appears to be. Strength-language can never give us this ability. The world and all its priorities are illusory; like mirages which trick us into making life-ending deviations... or a stone bridge in an action movie so well camouflaged as to be virtually invisible.

There is just one reality. God has defined it. The prophets of old spoke of it. Jesus died and rose again to open a way for humanity to reach it. The Holy Spirit calls us to risk everything we have and are in order to seal ourselves to it. But, to effectively risk everything for the sake of the gospel, we need nourishment. This is where I will next take us. The seventh habit of the spiritually tough is found in becoming spiritually fed.

8

Habit #7: Be Spiritually Fed

Being spiritually fed is more than just reading God's holy words, but let us begin there.

Whether or not you enjoy eating, I think you will agree with me that your body appreciate food. And as silly as it may be to point this out, we are what we eat.[1] Moreover, this observation about eating is just as relevant when it comes to being spiritually fed. In fact, being well-fed spiritually — we are told below — is more important than being physically nourished:

"A person does not live by bread alone, but by every word that comes from the mouth of God" (Matthew 4:4 quoting Deuteronomy 8:3).

That was Jesus quoting from a speech by Moses warning the Israelites to not forget about God when times are good. Jesus used those same words to counter Satan's first temptation as Jesus wandered in the desert for forty days after undergoing baptism by his cousin John.

Let us assume the words God speaks to humanity are essential for our continued wellbeing. The obvious next question then is, "Where do we find these nourishing words?" For those who follow the three great monotheistic religions — Judaism, Christianity, and Islam — the Bible is commonly accepted as containing God's word. Which words in particular within the Bible are God's may be a source of dispute, but there is broad agreement among these three faiths that biblical texts are to be held in high esteem. Hold onto that thought and focus on the idea that in order to be spiritually fed, the Bible is a good place to begin.

Because I myself am Christian, I am going to be speaking about being spiritually fed from this perspective. I am not ignoring or otherwise dishonoring these other faiths, I am just speaking from a place of knowledge and experience. If you happen not to be Christian, hopefully you will be able to translate this particular habit of spiritual toughness into your own religious context.

The Bible is a collection of books. Most Protestant versions have sixty-six of them between the Old and New Testaments. Catholic Bibles includes a few more. But, no matter which Bible we might pick up to read, they all share one common trait: every book of the Bible is a translation derived from ancient documents none of which is the original text.[2] And especially when it comes to the Old Testament, many of these books were written down only after existing first as an oral tradition for many centuries.

Another difficulty is that not all ancient texts are in agreement in some very important places.[3] As it pertains to us becoming spiritually fed, this means we should surround ourselves with as many different translations of the Bible as we can. Since there exists not even one original document, we need to focus instead on what we do have and trust it will be sufficient in meeting our spiritual needs.

Once we have a variety of Bibles in front of us, the next step is to read. There is simply no substitute for reading; or listening, if it is easier for you to hear the Bible being read by someone else. Either way, we need to make space in our lives for a personal encounter with God's holy words. Ideally, we should do this on a daily basis.

Just as our bodies were formed so we would need to take in oxygen and expel carbon dioxide, so too were we made to take in God's holy words and then let go of every worthless thought or idea. When we deny ourselves food, our bodies die of starvation. When we cease taking in God's holy words, our spirit — soul, if you prefer — becomes depleted and also dies. Perhaps we have been operating by the world's strength-language for as long as we can remember. Maybe we have intuitively understood the limits of strength-language and have instead been drawn to the ways of spiritual toughness. Either way, it is possible to feel like something is missing from our life.

If we are burdened by a sense of emptiness or of being incomplete, we are likely feeling the effects of spiritual malnourishment. One man likened this phenomena to reading a restaurant menu but failing to order any food![4] Many people seek after drugs or alcohol as ways to fill this void. But as AA participants remind themselves every week, going down that road is a losing strategy.[5] Reading the Bible may not encompass everything there is about becoming spiritually fed, but it is a good first step and far less expensive than beer, cigarettes, and street drugs.

Find someone who is a good source of biblical instruction.

There is a modern proverb which goes: "Every man who is his own lawyer, has a fool for a client."[6] Well, the same is true for the person who would try to be self-taught in terms of God's holy words. Just like playing tennis against a better opponent improves our own game, we must seek after someone who knows more about Scripture than we do and learn from them. After all, this isn't exactly a new idea:

"Now there was an Ethiopian eunuch, a court official of the Candace, queen of the Ethiopians, in charge of her treasury. He had come to Jerusalem to worship and was returning home; seated in his chariot, he was reading the prophet Isaiah. Then the Spirit said to Philip, 'Go over to this chariot and join it.' So Philip ran up to it and heard him reading the prophet Isaiah. He asked, 'Do you understand what you are reading?' He replied, 'How can I, unless someone guides me?'" (Acts 8:27-31)

Or, how about this:

"Woe to you, blind guides, who say, 'Whoever swears by the sanctuary is bound by nothing, but whoever swears by the gold of the sanctuary is bound by the oath.' You blind fools! For which is greater, the gold or the sanctuary that has made the gold sacred?" (Matthew 23:16-17)

Clearly, both the desire for good biblical instruction and the problem of really bad spiritual guidance have been around for a long time. This being the case, how are we to pick out the good guides from the bad ones? It turns out it isn't all that difficult: we must flee as fast as we can from any person who speaks about his or her religion using strength-language. These people are the "blind guides" of our time. We need to leave them in our dust. In fact, we might want to shake off that dust before we remove ourselves from their toxic influence.

Now, find some priest, rabbi, pastor, or imam who is talking about God using the language of spiritual toughness. Believe me, they exist and will be more than thrilled for you to ask them about any aspect of God's holy words. If our desire is to be spiritually fed, then finding a good guide is where we gather our plate and utensils in preparation of taking our place in the buffet line.

Consuming God's holy words is exactly like eating food and drink.

The next time you are at home or in a restaurant sitting at a table with food in front of you, make note of how you go about eating. Do you eat just one thing on your plate at a time before moving on to the next item? Do you mix everything together into one confused mess and chow down? Are you someone who doesn't really care? I did this exercise and it was very revealing.

Unless we are dining with royalty (or with our in-laws), there is not really a right or wrong way to eat. The reason I bring this up is to point out the way in which we eat a four-course meal often reveals how we might also consume God's words. Other than using knives, forks, spoons, and a napkin at the end, there is not much difference in how we feed our spirits as compared to how we feed our bodies. Come to think of, we should hold onto that napkin. We might need it to wipe the sweat from our brows after reading the Bible!

Just as with eating food, I do not believe there is a right or wrong way to take in God's holy words. What is needed is a way of interacting with them which makes sense to us personally. Is it better to do our Bible reading in the morning or the evening? Should we place Bible commentaries or other textual aides at our disposal and, if so, which ones? Do we prefer skipping around from New to Old Testament or would we rather just begin with Genesis and end with The Revelation of Saint John? Do we prefer reading alone or with one other person? Maybe we like to be among a group of like-minded searchers.

These are questions only we can answer for ourselves with perhaps some input from a scriptural guide. Our guide may see in us a need we ourselves have not yet identified. We must dare to trust this outside opinion because it could be the Holy Spirit speaking to us through that person. This is because consuming God's holy words and digesting them are not the same thing. But remember this also: A guide can only suggest where we should go. He or she cannot take that step for us, nor should they even try.

And that can be confirmation we are in the company of a genuine biblical expert. A competent guide shows us where our road of faith begins and does not expect us to follow in his or her footsteps. We are in this world to make a unique and personal spiritual journey (or not) to God. No one else can go on this journey for us, and there are no other options available apart from these two choices.

The buffet we call Scripture is always open and a clean plate always awaits us.

The habit of being spiritually fed is just that: a habit. It is not some event or other one-time happening. Here is something from the Bible which speaks to what I'm saying:

"But as for you, continue in what you have learned and have firmly believed, knowing from whom you learned it and how from childhood you have been acquainted with the sacred writings, which are able to make you wise for salvation through faith in Christ Jesus. All Scripture is breathed out by God and profitable for teaching, for reproof, for correction, and for training in righteousness, that the [person] of God may be competent, equipped for every good work" (2 Timothy 3:14-17) [bracketed word is mine].

The first recipient of this advice was a young preacher by the name of Timothy. The apostle Paul wrote those words to him sometime around the sixth decade of the first century of the Christian Era. And we could safely bet everything we own Paul never in his wildest dreams thought these words to Timothy would be included in that body of literature he called "sacred writings".

What Paul meant by this term was the Jewish Bible. Take a moment to let this sink in: The first few generations of Christians came to faith being spiritually fed by what we (erroneously) call the Old Testament because no one had yet written what we (also erroneously) call the New Testament. This bisection of the Bible is an ancient human construct which remains unsupported by the witness of Scripture itself.

There is, in point of fact, only one testament; one gospel; one story of humanity's salvation. "All Scripture is breathed out by God," says Paul to Timothy. We must understand to what Paul is referring. He is pointing his young colleague, and us, back to the story of humanity's creation in the book of Genesis where God breathed life into the man (in Genesis 2:7, this human does not yet have a name).[7]

The purpose in consuming of all these revealed words from God now becomes clear: Paul is telling Timothy they are to be for us a daily infusion of God's Holy Spirit. God, in other words, considers these holy words to be just as important, if not more so, to our earthly wellbeing as the very air (spirit) God breathed into the first human's lungs.

How many times a day do we take in a breath of air? Care to make a guess? How about as many as 500 times? Sorry, but that's not nearly enough. Well, then, how about 10,000 times? Nope, still too few. Try, on average, 22,320 times in the course of twenty-four hours.[8] Now multiply this figure by the number of days we have been on this planet. Then compare this final number with the number of times we have read the Bible or other sacred writings. On second thought, we shouldn't bother. Everyone in the world falls short in this comparison.

And, it is not even a fair comparison to begin with. Reading God's holy words just one time has far more impact on our spirits than many years of breathing has on our bodies. Just as it is never too late to get rid of a bad habit, it is also never too late to acquire a good one. In this case, reading God's holy words.

But, we must take our time. Read some sacred writings and let those holy words be understood by our hearts and minds; with assistance, if possible. Then, tomorrow, grab another clean plate from the buffet line and serve up another portion of some good, God-breathed nourishment. Make this activity a daily habit and remember that the source of our spiritual wellbeing is always available to us.

Prayer is another important way of becoming spiritually fed.

Take a moment and have a conversation with God whether or not you believe he exists. Prayer has been shown to significantly increase the overall health of believers as compared to people who claim no faith. So, it turns out there is a practical side to belief: It makes a difference in our physical wellbeing whether someone is an atheist or devoted believer.[9]

Still, the Creator of the universe is an equal-opportunity listener. Faith in God is not a precondition for prayer. This might have something to do with the fact — from God's lofty perspective — we humans are basically all in the same boat. Remember the stuff way back near the beginning of this book about everyone falling short of God's glory? That is why this is true. But, the important point here is God listens to us. Our personal opinion of God has no impact on his existence or on his willingness to hear us when we pray.

But, the benefits of prayer are undeniable. So, go ahead and pray to God. Pray even if you refrain from using the word "god" in your prayer. Pray because the point of prayer is for us to speak about what is weighing heavy on our spirit.

The dominant action in prayer is one of release.

If reading sacred writings is akin to breathing in God's Holy Spirit, prayer is how we exhale — how we clear ourselves in preparation of repeating the process. There is not one bodily function we possess which does not involve the action of releasing something back into the universe. Why, then, do many of us ignore the necessary release available through prayer?

There are developmentally disabled people who become frightened whenever they have to go to the restroom. They try to retain the stuff in their bladders or in their bowels, and often do so until some explosive event overtakes them.[10] People who choose not to pray are committing this very same mistake in terms of their spirituality. Eventually some emotional event overtakes their lives. Believe me when I say such a moment is the worst time to start up a chat with God. Oh, God doesn't have a problem with it, but we might not be bringing our best selves to the conversation.

This is why we need the discipline of daily prayer. We are human beings. This means there is a lot of nasty stuff coursing through us every day only a fraction of which is meant to be flushed down a toilet. If we don't pray, then we cannot release the vast majority of it; which means it stays inside us building up all sorts of pressure on our bodies, minds, and spirits.

For goodness sake, pray! Pray and experience the natural release of your fears, pains, and disappointments. It doesn't matter whether or not you believe God will take them from you (he will). What matters is you have given them up in the manner you were created to purge them.

In the act of praying, we also create an empty space for God to fill with his love.

Releasing our anxieties in prayer often triggers another powerful means of becoming spiritually fed because we have now made spiritual space available for God to fill with what he knows we need: the power of his love. Often what fills the void left behind when we pray away our problems is a mysterious and profound sense that we ought to do something for someone else. Again, we need look no further than to our own bodies for an analogy as to what is going on.

The reason we respire is so oxygen can be stripped from the air and transferred to every cell in our bodies to serve the process of cellular combustion. This combustion produces the carbon dioxide we exhale. In between all this breathing in and breathing out is where we accumulate the power to get our daily work done. God is ready to provide to our spirits what the process of breathing gives to our bodies. This power is called the love of God. But we can't obtain it unless we are willing to engage in spiritual nourishment.

Perhaps you feel as if God is withholding from you the power of his love. Understand this: God has given us the freedom even to reject him. If you and I aren't engaging in daily prayer, then we must not blame God. Our rejection of God makes it impossible for us to benefit from the love he is ever-ready to share with us. Our continued and persistent spiritual malnourishment is gumming up the works!

Worshipping with a community of like-minded believers is another way.

Adamant atheists and frequent worshippers alike may choose to skip or, at best, skim-over this next section. Those committed to regular worship will likely encounter little information here they don't already know. As for atheists, what can I say except that, unlike prayer, worship insists we direct our actions toward a Supreme Being. But, if you don't believe in God, there is not much point in learning how you can be spiritually fed through regular worship.

This section is especially relevant for people like those making up the vast majority of Americans: Folk who believe in God but who hardly ever attend a worship service. I won't waste time reciting a list of the most-common reasons why this population stays away from houses of worship. What I will speak on are two important ways worship feeds the human spirit. They are not, I assure you, the only ones.

I am going to begin with a practical consideration noted long ago by essayist John Donne: we are connectional creatures. The human soul is fed or starved depending on the proximity of our relationships. One of us can't long exist apart from the rest of us in the same way one of our body parts cannot survive amputation unless it is reattached. Furthermore, we who remain are diminished when that one falls or is cut away. As Donne said so eloquently, "No man is an island entire of itself; every man is a piece of the continent, a part of the main."[11]

For the believer who nevertheless abstains from worship, the practical effect is twofold: the adoration of God is diminished due to the loss of even one voice; and as long as he or she remains amputated from the larger body of like-minded folk, the absent believer deprives himself or herself of the unique spiritual food which may be obtained only within that sustained liturgical relationship.

(For those of us who believe in God, it should go without saying he expects us to venerate him on a regular basis — if for no other reason than to show him our gratitude. But, that is a discussion for another time and another book. The point of this section is to focus on how worship feeds us.)

The second consideration concerns the power available to us from an authentic worship experience. This energy is the spiritual equivalent of climbing to the top of a barren hill during a thunderstorm and lifting high our arms to the possibility of being struck by lightning. That is how dynamic an experience worshipping with like-minded believers can be.

Now, here is a potential concern: Worship isn't always going to strike us this way, nor should we expect it to. Just because we raise our arms in adoration to God is no guarantee of becoming a spiritual lightning rod. Remember, we aren't the only ones at the top of that hill. And even though it is a human endeavor, God controls every aspect of worship.

But, from time to time, the moment, the music, and the message all combine to make that day's worship experience something to remember. The bolt hits us and we come away with an insight which completely changes the arc of our lives. Most of the time, though, our presence is needed to facilitate someone else's mountaintop experience. The Holy

Spirit cannot be constrained, and we have no idea the effect our presence in worship may be having on those around us. But if we don't climb the hill, we absolutely (and selfishly, I might add) reduce someone else's opportunity to be awe-struck and we eliminate ours altogether.

The spiritual nourishment available in worship is unique. Of the three ways I have mentioned, it is the only activity impossible to do alone. The veneration of God only happens in a group setting. And in that truth is found both the power of religious relationships and the terrible cost of isolating ourselves from such a spiritually fulfilling opportunity.

We are each responsible for our own spiritual nourishment.

Perhaps you have tried strategies other than reading God's holy words, group worship, and prayer as ways of feeding your spirit. I know what that looks like, because I wasn't always an ordained minister. I also know there comes a time in the life of most of us when we come face to face with this truth: The way we have been seeking after our spiritual wellbeing just isn't working. Addictions only serve to enlarge the voids we sought to fill; seeking thrills and defying death inevitably leads to a place where not enough suddenly becomes too much; denial is a losing strategy; and it is always painful when we slip on our karma and fall flat on our hubris.

At some point in time we just need to stop. We need to stop trying to make it through life on our own steam. We absolutely must stop trying to be strong, for heaven's sake! If not for heaven's sake, then how about for our own sake? You are the only one who can provide you with spiritual nourishment. Read God's holy words. Engage in daily prayer. Attend a worship service with like-minded believers. Make room for God to fill you with the power of his love. Be spiritually fed. These habits are what tough people all over the world do so they can face the hardships of life.

And while each of us is in the buffet line, we should consider inviting someone else to join us. Heck, we might even suggest they cut ahead of us. Why should we do this? Because the next habit of the spiritually tough is forged when we both encourage and enjoy the success of others.

9

Habit #8: Encourage and Enjoy the Success of Others

Strong-minded people tend to be jealous of the success of others.

I have been in pastoral ministry long enough to hear just about every kind of relationship problem known to exist. One of the most heart-breaking for me is where one person (usually a woman) describes how controlling and unsupportive her partner or spouse is. It doesn't take long to figure out — if it is the underlying cause — that the more strong-minded person in the pair is jealous of his partner's perceived success compared to what he has achieved. Envy is one of strength-language's saddest, most insidious, and destructive consequences. Since strength-language creates the need for winners and losers, there exists in its philosophy little room in the strong-minded person for fostering or even enjoying the success of a peer lest this other person be seen as gaining ground on or attaining a place of dominance over them.[1]

It has been my observation that jealousy is often exhibited by people desperate to win by any means possible. For this reason alone, it has no place in the life of any person claiming to have faith in God. Indeed, the degree to which we exhibit envy is a good indicator of yet how far we need to go in our spiritual maturing.

I regret and feel shame for the damage left behind by my outbursts of jealousy. I hope you do, too. We may not be able to undo all the pain caused by our envy over some other person's achievement. However, real hope is found when we discard the strength-language which has given jealousy this ability to create havoc in our lives in the first place.

The eighth habit of spiritual toughness asks us to model the emotional state which is jealousy's polar opposite. For Christians, we are able to make this radical turn-around (think repentance) because we accept the victory which is already ours by grace through faith in Jesus Christ. Has any of us ever heard of the victor in a contest being jealous? No, nobody has. Winners are too busy expressing emotions like joy to have either the time or the inclination to be jealous. The man or woman who claims to be a person of faith and yet still harbors envy has a problem on his or her hands: they are in deep spiritual bondage.

The time has come to free ourselves from this spiritual bondage.

If we find ourselves comparing our achievements to our co-workers, family members, or even to our spouse, this is yet more evidence we are enslaved by the world's strength-language. Recall that the other possible ways the world — or, if you prefer, Satan — has accomplished our bondage is by tempting us to: 1) be unwilling to embrace the changes going on around us; 2) focus on control; 3) ignore God's call; 4) be crippled by our sins; 5) feel entitlement; 6) be risk-averse, and; 7) be spiritually malnourished.

By now — if we have been looking at our faith-life journey with a sober eye — we should have arrived at the following conclusion: Basing our relationship with God on concepts revolving around spiritual strength has given us nothing but grief. Included in this litany of sorrows may be our envy of people who have a more satisfying relationship with God, or who have greater success in the area of faith development than we have heretofore experienced. Before any of us goes into some sort of spiritual tail-spin, we should consider this story:

"In the course of time Cain brought to the Lord an offering of the fruit of the ground, and Abel also brought of the firstborn of his flock and of their fat portions. And the Lord had regard for Abel and his offering, but for Cain and his offering he had no regard. So Cain was very angry and his face fell" (Genesis 4:3-5).

The tale of Cain's jealousy and anger ends with his brother Abel's blood crying out to God from the ground, and with Cain's banishment and prominent feature (the mark of Cain) to protect him from harm. In truth, you and I are no better at ruling over our sin than Cain was at ruling over his. Likewise, we are responsible for the way in which we comport ourselves to family and friends, to the rest of humanity, and in any hoped-for relationship with God.

You and I have both the opportunity and the responsibility to embrace the habits of spiritual toughness and thereby be freed from the envy which does nothing but empower unholy desires. Maybe we cannot control our sin, be we can darn well manage it better than we have up to now.

Spiritually tough people look for opportunities to help other people shine.

Just think how different the Cain and Abel story would have turned out if Cain had been living his life by the habits of spiritual toughness instead of by strength-language. Cain could have celebrated his brother's acceptable offering instead of plotting to eliminate a rival he blamed for harming his relationship with God by being better at showing gratitude.

Spiritually strong people like Cain believe God's favor is somehow limited in quantity. They must think this way, for then why be jealous of someone else's accomplishments in this life to begin with? In contrast, spiritually tough people know God's love to be unlimited such that there always will be more than enough of his favor to go around.

But because the spiritually strong person believes God's favor to be finite, he or she seeks to control how much of it goes elsewhere. And because the strong-minded person can't control the source of this gracious love, he or she resorts instead to interfering with those who receive it.

Cain's way of looking at himself, the world around him, and God was completely bankrupt. The same is true of all who seek after God in a similar manner. However, the person who operates on the basis of spiritual toughness understands the success of those around him or her — not just in terms of faith, but in every aspect — actually benefits instead of threatens his or her own wellbeing. For this reason alone, the spiritually tough person is more apt to seek after ways of fostering those successes. What follows is a great example of what I'm talking about.

Mary Kay Ash began something in 1963 that no other woman had ever before tried: She created a profitable cosmetics company from the grass roots while at the same time she empowered millions of women (and even some men) the world over to succeed beyond their wildest dreams.[2] How did she do this? She set into motion a business model whereby directors would encourage and empower a sales force called "consultants" who would each have their own client base and the opportunity to work hard enough to themselves become a director.

Success for these consultants was designed to translate into success for their mentor. Knowing this created incentives for each director to teach and train her consultants to be the best they could be at selling Mary Kay products. And each consultant knew she was supported, not undermined, by the others in her geographic region.

Mary Kay Ash was a woman of deep faith in God. Her motto was, "God first, family second, and career third."[3] I believe she was also someone who intuitively understood the importance of operating by spiritual toughness instead of by spiritual strength. There was — and still is — no room in her company for internal rivalries or jealousy. After all, it would be bad for business. Every Mary Kay director knows it to be absolutely true she shines all the brighter the more she encourages the success of those under her care and training. In my way of thinking, there is no better contemporary example of this eighth habit of spiritual toughness than the over 1.6 million Mary Kay consultants living out their success all around the world.[4]

Strength language is about the charity of giving someone a fish.

We have all heard the adage about giving someone a fish and understand how this daily supply of food results in a relationship of dependency between receiver and giver. Now is the time we name this dynamic for what it really is: control born from envy but disguised as love. It is a dynamic which occupies many twisted and brutal chapters in both American and World History.[5]

As most of us know, slaves living in Dixie prior to the American Civil War were not permitted an education. This was a deliberate strategy designed to keep them ignorant and less able to effect their escape from bondage. It also made them dependent upon the white society which had total control over their lives.[6] This wasn't the first time a specific population had had their freedoms stripped from them in such an unjust and blatantly sinful manner:

"Now there arose a new king over Egypt, who did not know Joseph. And he said to his people, 'Behold, the people of Israel are too many and too mighty for us. Come, let us deal shrewdly with them, lest they multiply, and, if war breaks out, they join our enemies and fight against us and escape from the land'" (Exodus 1:8-10).

90

Can you hear the desire for control in those words? Do you sense the fear? There is also a smattering of jealousy in the observation there are too many Israelites; as if by some magic the Egyptians were being prevented from procreating! Do not for one minute think such sentiments are dead and buried under the sands of North Africa. These types of fears, this desire to control, and the blatant jealousies are, sadly, alive and well in our century and in just about every country on this planet.

They are present wherever anyone's civil rights are being curtailed. They are there wherever a person is being paid in an illegal manner or at a rate which cannot sustain his or her life. They are present in any level of government which earns its income by fleecing the very people those elected officials each took an oath to serve and protect. It exists in any judicial system which profits by turning drug addicts into assets of the prison system. These are all examples of twenty-first century slavery. Oh, and it also exists where there is a child whose parents do not care if he or she gets an education, or whether that same child is in the next room while his or her parents cook their next batch of methamphethamine.[7]

Here is an important observation which should be universally accepted: Beware the person or group who is very good at handing out fish but shows little desire to teach someone how to do his or her own fishing. These folk often appear to be very generous and even loving as they say things like, "And I've often wondered, are they better off as slaves, picking cotton and having a family life and doing things, or are they better off under government subsidy? They didn't get no more freedom. They got less freedom."[8]

Such people are filled with fear as they fling around their strength-language like a club. They are — just like the ancient Egyptians — afraid of being murdered in their beds by the people they are busy oppressing. Even worse in their twisted thinking, they are afraid of being eclipsed, marginalized, and eventually one day being forgotten by the history books.

And remember also what we learned from the Cain and Abel story: the humble, down-trodden people of this world — to their envious and powerful brothers — become rivals for God's affection and therefore must be eliminated like Abel was; and like European Jews were during the

Second World War; and like African-Americans are still experiencing to this day.

But, there can be no love present in a relationship based on dependency, and no salvation to be found in its philosophy of strength and control. In the end, the bondage and oppression the strong-minded would seek to force onto others becomes the very chains which seal their own doom. This, too, is the word of the Lord, and not merely my opinion.[9]

The language of spiritual toughness is about the charity of teaching someone how to fish.

Unless we are ready to share our accumulated wisdom and life-experiences with others, it is difficult for me to comprehend how we can do anything other than hand out fish.

(By-the-way, do not confuse what I am criticizing here with "philanthropy." Philanthropy is a form of generosity which is itself a specialized habit of the spiritually tough. However, the action of "handing out fish" is surface charity designed more to make the giver look good than to solve any problems on the receiving end of the transaction.)

Teaching someone a skill is an intimate act. We must get close enough to that other person to risk being bothered by her shampoo or his deodorant. To teach is to empathize with them; with his problems or her limitations. Explaining how an internal combustion engine operates, how to solve algebraic equations, or how that other person can tumble on a floor mat without breaking his or her neck are all acts of love disguised as teaching. In teaching, we surrender any desire to control the relationship: it is a collaborative effort.

Have you ever wondered why Jesus was so focused on educating his disciples about the kingdom of heaven? Well, he didn't become human just to sit on the sidelines. Christ came to teach us how to value having a relationship with God by teaching things like this:

"'The kingdom of heaven is like a treasure hidden in a field, which a man found and covered up. Then in his joy he goes and sells all that he has and buys that field. Again, the kingdom of heaven is like a merchant in search of fine pearls, who, on finding one pearl of great value, went and sold all he had and bought it. Again, the kingdom of heaven is like a net that was thrown into the sea and gathered fish of every kind. When it was full, men drew it ashore and sat down and sorted the good into containers but threw away the bad'" (Matthew 13:44-48).

As instructive as these parables are, the most important lesson Jesus taught about the nature of heaven he delivered while nailed to a tree. He taught anyone with ears enough to hear and eyes enough to see that if we trust God, death becomes an impossibility for us. Jesus — in his own body — demonstrated how toughness was a far more important quality to have than strength.

But his crucifixion was much more than an act of performance art, though no doubt many Gentile and Jewish observers that sad day found entertainment on the slopes of Golgotha. Jesus died so you and I might live out our faith with the power of God's own strength rather than cast about in a scum-pond of our own power. That, and to pass on lessons like this one:

"'This is my commandment, that you love one another as I have loved you. Greater love has no one than this, that someone lay down his life for his friends'" (John 15:12-13).

Deriving enjoyment from watching others succeed should be as natural to us as breathing.

This is one habit of spiritual toughness which should be as easy as learning how to ride a bicycle. People with children should understand what I'm talking about. Before we go about teaching our kids how to do it, we often have to recall the mechanics of riding one. Only then do we feel confident enough to instruct them to the point where they get to remove the training wheels. Confident, but also anxious!

What is parenthood, after all, if not moments of trepidation followed by joy as we watch our children succeed over and over again as they grow and mature? Any parent who does not live for these precious moments might just as well stop claiming to be one altogether.

Most parents (just to let you non-parents in on a secret) ache to see their children succeed. When they don't, it ruins our sleep. When they do, we breathe ten times easier. How is it possible, then, that we neglect to apply this same attitude to everyone else? Perhaps there is some kind of primal clan filter at work in us which makes difficult — if not impossible — our enjoyment of the success of potential rivals.

Consider what has happened throughout history when a king determined his own children to be a threat to his power. If a person can kill his own kin so as to remove a perceived threat, then that person could hardly be expected to enjoy watching someone outside his family succeed. Are some modern-day parents so envious of the opportunities their children have to succeed that they do everything in their power to eliminate either the chances or the children?

If we look at our lives and conclude we simply cannot enjoy the success of our children — let alone anyone else — this is further evidence we are thinking and deciding and living under the influence of the world's strength-language. Now is perhaps a good time to highlight this small but important passage from the Bible:

"...and with the measure you use it will be measured to you" (Matthew 7:2).

In the context of this chapter, the commodity being measured-out is the habit of taking pleasure in watching other people shine. Since this action is itself a kind of judgment, the above quote is a thoroughly relevant passage. Jesus promises us — no matter what we happen to be trading in — if our scales are generous, this same generosity will be applied to us when it is our turn to be judged. Conversely, if our way of measuring others is not generous, then this same lack of generosity will govern the way in which God examines the sum total of our lives.

Is it reasonable for us to imagine God takes pleasure in our success when we have neglected to do the same in the lives of his other children? The answer, of course, is no. If we cannot find the fortitude crucial in learning this habit of spiritual toughness, we are sunk in terms of our eternal existence. As long as we continue to operate using spiritual strength, we have little hope of switching out our stingy scales for a more generous set.

Our lives are a continual process of determining what is important and what isn't. If we do this in an honest manner, then we must conclude everyone deserves the opportunity to succeed. But as long as strength-language is allowed to dominate our thinking, we are actively working against this hope.

When we operate using the language of spiritual toughness, we no longer see the success of others as a threat to our own wellbeing. We can be like parents who gush with joy at their child's first steps, or who cry a river as they watch that same kid graduate from university, get married, or succeed far beyond the parent's own ability to do so.

What I know to be true is this: In acquiring this particular habit of spiritual toughness we are sacrificing something I call the pride of our personal success. However, this pride is something we no longer need if we accept the truth of our salvation coming through Jesus Christ; the same Jesus who:

"...though he was in the form of God, did not count equality with God a thing to be grasped, but made himself nothing, taking on the form of a servant, being born in the likeness of men. And being found in human form, he humbled himself by becoming obedient to the point of death, even death on a cross" (Philippians 2:6-8).

It can be argued sacrificing our pride of personal success for the sake of others is much easier than sacrificing the hatred we feel for our enemies. I would agree with anyone who believed this. Still, you had to know it was coming: The ninth habit of the spiritually tough is found when we practice loving those who are — in our personal estimation — unlovable.

10

Habit #9: Love the Unlovable

Hate is the default emotion wherever strength-language reigns supreme.

Just as a person might say he or she was born with a particular sexual orientation, most of us are born with the complete palate of human emotions including hatred.[1] Hate (and those emotional states closely linked to it) is in us because it is a necessary components of what it means to be human. Hate was not and has never been some evolutionary error or evidence of a mistake on God's part.[2]

Now, there are many other qualities which help define us: our capacity for kindness, our ability to create written language, or our humor and propensity for play. But for the purposes of this chapter, I would like to focus on emotions and, in particular, the ones we call hatred and love.

One obvious function of hatred is self-preservation. A person will almost always feel hatred when he or she recognizes someone has been aggressive toward them or even attacked them or someone close to them. Similar to the body's ability to feel physical pain caused by some malady or injury, hatred is often the consequence of emotional pain. Our ability to hate makes us more aware of potential danger and it may even help us identify who might be a source of that threat. Finally, hate helps us to retaliate against our enemies (real or imagined) and, for this reason, it is the preferred emotional state of those who operate by strength-language.

Recall that back at the beginning of this book, I spoke "about vectors of power" and how strength and toughness differed in terms of what that power was being used to do. I said the power inherent in spiritual toughness was mostly defensive and protective and reflective, whereas the energy in spiritual strength tended to be aggressive and offensive.

If any emotional state could be said to be the world's default choice, it must be hatred.[3] And because most of us don't understand how we have been conned, taught, lied to, and pressured into using the world's strength-language, we react to the hate of others by projecting our own aggression. As a consequence, hate and enmity become looped into reflexive cycles of misery all the while well-meaning people wring their hands and say things like: "What can we do? This is how we are made."

Human beings are among the least lovable creatures in the world.

Just because we were made to feel hatred does not mean we must automatically act on it whenever it rises up in us. We have other choices. In fact, attitudes like "I can't help it," or "He made me hit him" make human beings among the least lovable creatures in the world. Believing we are unable to curb the consequences of our emotional pain, or thinking just because we feel hatred, we have a right to act on this emotion are false justifications which become like dry forest underbrush: fuel for the fires of human conflict. Here is an example from long ago of what I am talking about:

"Now when they heard these things [from Stephen] they were enraged, and they ground their teeth at him. But he, full of the Holy Spirit, gazed into heaven and saw the glory of God, and Jesus standing at the right hand of God. But they cried out with a loud voice and stopped their ears and rushed together at him. Then they cast him out of the city and stoned him" (Acts of the Apostles 7:54-55, 57-58) [bracketed words are mine].

Stephen was martyred because a group of angry men permitted their collective rage to run rampant. They committed murder all the while saying, "This man's prophetic vision made us do it!" Such a rationalization is as bogus today as it was back then. But, the really amazing thing about this episode was how Stephen responded to their hatred. He said: "Lord, do not hold this sin against them."[4]

Stephen found a way to stop perpetuating the cycle of hatred and violence by loving the unlovable. It was a way first forged by God himself. Did that last quote from young, bold Stephen seem familiar? Well, it would be if we recall the part in the Gospel of Luke about the killing of Jesus. Stephen repeated almost word for word what the Lord spoke from atop the cross. Christ, before he died, asked his Father to forgive the sins of the Romans who crucified him, the Jewish officials who condemned him, and the populace (including his disciples) who abandoned him.

That request from Jesus was one of the final steps in God's plan of paving the one and only pathway to love the unlovable creatures he had been trying *not* to exterminate since he banished Adam and Eve from the Garden of Eden. Other parts of this plan involved Jesus' descent into hell and his bodily resurrection. Together, these actions formed the basis of a contract God forged with himself; a contract executed through Jesus' obedience even unto an unjust death.

Here are two important things to know: the first is God experiences hate and is quite capable of acting on his hatred; the second is that atonement for sin requires a blood sacrifice. Together, they combine to form God's justice; and by rights we are the ones who should be doing the bleeding. Yet ever since people discovered how to sin against him, God has been crafting the way of not permitting his justifiable rage to burn against us. This is God's love, but we have no right to expect it from him. It is his gift to us, not something we are owed or can earn. If nothing else in this life, we ought to understand these paired truths.

Earlier in his speech, Stephen gave the Sanhedrin a synopsis of Israel's prophetic history in which he said pretty much every prophet God sent to his people was abused and/or murdered.[5] These vocal visionaries were among the first elements of God's plan of salvation. It would have been nice if their efforts had been met with more of a positive response. Alas, God's plan would have to go to the ultimate mile:

"But God shows his love for us in that while we were still sinners, Christ died for us" (Romans 5:8).

What the apostle Paul expressed above in his letter to the Roman church is the basis for a concept Christians theologians call "unconditional love."[6] It is a simple idea God uses as a tactic of last resort. After a long string of strategies which tried to bring humanity back into fellowship with him, unconditional love is the one solution God knew would succeed. Why is that? How could God be sure the death of his Christ would work whereas everything else God had tried did not? The answer is this: it is the solution which does not rely on human actions.

In what is today commonly called the Old Testament — in those places where God is making covenants with his people — God uses the word if a lot.[7] These early covenants were conditioned on the behavior first of the Patriarchs and, then later, the Israelites. The amazing thing about these contracts was that God gave his people the possibility of not holding up their end of the bargain.

This profound freedom of choice also happens to be another of those qualities which help to define our humanity. Having the latitude to make our own decisions is wonderful for us, but becomes a problem for God because while God wants our decision to be with him to be genuine and uncoerced, he can't abide the presence of anyone or anything unholy.

Needless to say, God's people have proven themselves unable to hold up their end of these contracts. This frustrating consequence of human freedom is what prompted the writer of Psalm 14 to observe, "…there is none who does good, not even one." No matter how willing our spirit may be to obey the Lord, sin insures not one of us is able to use our God-given freedom to perfectly seek after him. This is why any means of human salvation which involves human effort is doomed to failure.

But, in asking people to have faith in the death and resurrection of Jesus Christ, God created the opportunity for us to stand before him in holiness. He detached our inability to be holy from his requirements which lead to salvation. God doesn't wait for us to accomplish something we can't. Nor does he ask us to atone for our sins knowing we would never survive such a trial. Instead, he accomplishes our salvation for us and simply asks us to acknowledge and to trust in his act of unconditional love.

God left directions on how we can demonstrate unconditional love in our human relationships.

Now comes the really difficult part for both you and me: The necessary way of demonstrating we both understand and accept God's unconditional love in Christ is by emulating this same love in our own lives. Wow! Couldn't God have asked us to do something just a bit easier? I don't know… like learning how to breathe underwater without the aid of a scuba tank? Unfortunately, God wants us to show him we get it. He wants you and me to love those unlovable creatures of the world called human beings.

Moreover, he doesn't want us to wait to do this until these unlovable creatures gain some sort of personal insight and stop being quite so unlovable. This is why the ninth habit of the spiritually tough is all about practicing unconditional love. When it comes to this concept, we must be able to move beyond theory. The following snippet from Scripture provides us with one example of what this looks like:

101

"Jesus said to Simon Peter, 'Simon, son of John, do you love me more than these?' He said to him, 'Yes, Lord, you know that I love you.' He said to him, 'Feed my lambs'" (John 21:15).

I can already hear a multitude of voices asking me, "Pastor Truman, how am I supposed to do that in my life?" Well, my answer is to say, "Don't even go there." We must not pretend for a single second we don't already know how to "feed the Lord's lambs." Jesus left us a well-marked map to follow. The road is still there and all the signage is intact. No one has blown up any bridge or erected any barrier to prevent our passage. The only obstacle is our unwillingness to believe Jesus to be the embodiment of God's unconditional love. If Jesus could forgive Peter for denying him three times, what is there keeping us from showing this same kind of love to the unlovable people of the world? This is how we are to feed them.

To love unconditionally we must sacrifice our desires for strength, power, and control.

The only barrier to us taking the first steps down the road to a faith-life in God is our reliance on the world's strength-language. You can take this statement right to the faith-in-God bank and deposit it. A person might give any one of a dozen reasons why he or she doesn't believe in God; doesn't go to church; doesn't pray; why they feel jealous; or why they can't love unconditionally. But when we strip away all the pretense, what we find staring back at us is an unwillingness to embrace change; the desire to be in control; the need to feel entitled; blatant jealousy; or a desire to be vengeful.

I said it before and I'll say it again: continuing to operate using strength-language is like trying to run with thirty-pound weights around our ankles. The strategy of living by spiritual strength is for the person who, frankly, would rather shut the door to eternity with God than admit God has forged their salvation through his unconditional love.

The person who is taking the first steps down the road to a life of true faith in God must begin by sacrificing his or her need to place conditions on the love they are supposed to be sharing — especially in the way this love is shared with those whom they are estranged. We are called to do this because this is exactly how God found the only way to love the unlovable us: by turning his own rage against us onto his own self. In the crucifixion of Jesus Christ, God sacrificed his own hatred for humanity thereby enabling us to follow Jesus who is the first-born of the new creation.

So, we cannot play the ignorance card. Like God, we must be willing to sacrifice our own hatred rather than letting it burn against those we desperately need to be with. We kill our hatred by practicing unconditional love until it becomes habitual within us. And we practice unconditional love every day by waking up to this truth: God loved us while we were still unlovable sinners. Literally speaking, that message should be the first thing our eyes see upon opening each day.

Giving our hate permission to burn against those who have caused us emotional pain does not please God and it never will. But, God has shown amazing patience while he waits for us to figure this out for ourselves. This brings us to this book's final habit of spiritual toughness. We must be patient with ourselves and with others as we continue down the road to a life of faith in God.

11

Habit #10: Cultivate Patience

Just like it was with courage, it is best not to think of patience as a virtue.

Calling patience a virtue is like emphasizing the nutritional quality of broccoli in order to get our kids to eat it. Most kids today are too sophisticated to fall for this kind of hollow dodge. Therefore, labelling patience a virtue is about as effective a strategy of inducing it into someone as is teaching about the habits of an octopus by describing the habits of an elephant.

Therefore, I will be speaking about what patience is and isn't, not what it is *like*. I will explain why we need to begin being patient with ourselves when it comes to habituating it before we can be patient with others. Finally, I will give my rationale as to why cultivating patience is my final habit of the spiritually tough.

To repeat my initial thought, let us forget all that stuff about patience being a virtue. And while we are at it, we can also chuck aside the idea of patience as a strategy for getting our way; patience as a means to an end;

104

or patience as offering us some kind of window into another person's inner-workings.

Patience is an emotional, psychological, behavioral, linguistic, relational, religious, or even an intellectual pause.[1] It can be a denouement at times with an expiration date, or at other moments without a time limit. Patience, we are told by the apostle Paul, is also the first characteristic of love:

"Love is patient and kind; love does not boast; it is not arrogant or rude. It does not insist on its own way: it is not irritable or resentful" (1 Corinthians 13:4-5).

Patience is a pause both purposeful and active. It is as charitable as it is not accidental![2] In the previous chapter, I spoke about how the ninth habit of the spiritually tough is found in loving the unlovable. This being the case, the tenth habit is found in how well we wait while the focus of our unconditional love learns to habituate, like us, the habits of spiritual toughness. Patience only becomes a powerful tool in the hands of those who are able to wield it through this same spiritual toughness. This is why most strong-minded people fail at being patient: they can't or won't understand the power behind the pause.

Pausing is an action designed to remove us from the flow of time.

Habituating patience places us near God's perspective on the ebb and flow of history.[3] Being patient — as opposed to acting patient — is a non-linear action. To execute patience well, it should be done without expectations. Forget about the kitchen timer for this exercise. Our expectations are too often about anticipating an outcome the way we want it to be. But because patience places us outside the scope of all possible outcomes, we can only ever exist in the moment. At the very least, this is where our patience should remain.

Patience is not really patience unless we are willing to suspend our expectations that the person we are being asked to love unconditionally will somehow be changed by our actions. If we have tried to get closer to God so the soul of someone near and dear to us might be saved, then we have made a terrible mistake. Saving souls is God's business, and he gives everyone the same opportunity to come back to him or not. We should not be embarking on this journey of a life of faith in God for anyone but our own self.[4]

God is patient with us, so what is our excuse?

We are, however, blessed in that God is ever-patient, slow to anger, and overflowing in love. God will wait for us to stop using the world's strength-language in an attempt to wrestle our way to salvation. He also practices patience with us as we begin to incorporate the habits of spiritual toughness into our lives.

Throughout this book, I have been hinting at one very important component of our faith-development. Now, however, I am going to say it plainly. If God can be patient with us, what, then, is our excuse for not being patient with ourselves? We must stop berating ourselves for not having a closer relationship with God than we have been experiencing up to now. Developing a faith-life in God is difficult work made even more so by our doing it while using the false doctrine of the world's strength-language.

Remember, we have been duped, conned, and serenaded by things the world holds to be important: strength, power, and control among others. But, it takes only one courageous act of repentance to drive away these phantom priorities. Only then are we free to realign our thinking, deciding, and doing around habits of spiritual toughness. Because God has made faith to work in this manner, practicing patience may be the highest form of self-love.

As we begin down this new road of faith, we can dare merge onto this lane of patience where time, and the twin pressures to act and achieve are kept at bay. Remember that patience is not a permission to be lazy in our quest for a faith-life. Rather, it is an intentional pause along our journey to permit our obedience to catch up with our aspirations. When we move into an attitude of patience, we give God's love for us the ability to deepen our relationship with him. When we were operating by the world's strength-language, patience resembled more an unnecessary pit stop we were made to endure while getting to where we wanted to be.

Being patient with ourselves is the first step in our quest of being patient with others.

Only when we have gained success at being patient with ourselves can we then be patient with others. And while we may not want to be patient with other people, the hard truth is we need to be. Remember, patience is also the first characteristic of love. But if this is not enough of a reason, how about the fact many of those others have been supremely patient with us? It is important for us to remember this key fact: we more often begin our journey of faith by being the beneficiaries of some other person's loving pause.

At this moment, though, I want us to imagine each of us as the person providing the pause for others, and especially for those persons closest to us. As we do this we should have few illusions. This is an advanced form of faith development. Being patient combines many of the habits of spiritual toughness we have already learned about: the courage to embrace change; most certainly our need to switch from control-mindedness to managing our lives; gratitude is in there, too, as is the determination to risk everything our senses tell us are real and valuable.

107

Whenever the opportunity arises for us to be patient with the people we most love, remember these things: patience is not a tactic to help us acquire some desired outcome; and, it should never be used as a means to an end (it is an end in itself). We will know we have successfully added this habit of spiritual toughness to our lives when we find ourselves responding to the actions of others rather than reacting to them. Believe me, there is a difference. Reaction is a choice more often used by people who practice strength-language. Response is a choice which flows from faith, grace, love, and the language of spiritual toughness.

Our capacity for patience exists apart from the universe's rational laws and God's revealed laws.

Sir Isaac Newton's Third Law of Motion, when translated from the original Latin into English, begins, "To every action there is always opposed an equal reaction."[5] My take on this interaction of what physicists call force pairs[6] is to say it is the mathematical equivalent of "An eye for an eye and a tooth for a tooth."[7] As such, it is a principle lodged in strength-language.

Laws — whatever their source — leave no room for doing anything other than formulating conclusions based on the observable evidence. This means there is no concept of grace in mathematics; nor will a scientist ever wait for the foundational statutes of the universe to change to suit his or her theory. In the same vein, the Bible says there is no mercy under the law, only a vengeful judgment.[8]

From the universe's point of view, there are only our reactions to the actions which happen to us. We live in a physical realm dominated by the principles of force pairs. Then we make the mistake of trying to apply these same principles to our spirituality and wonder why we are so frustrated in our faith-walk.

(Which is why it is a far better thing to have people sit in judgment over people than to turn over such responsibility to pre-programed, inflexible sentencing guidelines. A human being free from these sort of restrictions knows the place of both patience and grace. Any legal system which denies mercy its proper role in a court of law ceases to be one which cares about justice.)

This confirms what I have long-suspected: our capacity for things like love and patience exists apart from either the universe's rational laws or God's revealed laws. Qualities like faith, love, and patience are like anti-matter inasmuch as they should not exist in this universe. Yet these qualities do exist. We know they do for we see their residual traces spinning all around us in oddly beautiful ARKs — like decay patterns formed from a collision of sub-atomic particles at CERN.

Which makes it important we use a language and a set of principles in our faith-walk just as alien to this world as anti-matter. I am convinced such a language is found in spiritual toughness where every habit we learn becomes as important as Quantum Mechanics is for the physicist whose observations and conclusions are confined to the arena of action and reaction.

The ability to cultivate patience is an important milestone of our faith development.

Responding to people who themselves are reacting badly to the changed way we are now practicing our faith is another matter. Assuming they have said or done something hurtful to us, ignoring this projection of power from them is not the answer. Using the apostle Paul's concepts underlying the "whole armor of God," we must meet strength with toughness. In the present context, this is knowing our patience with and love for the other person will deflect their aggression toward us.

Only when this has been accomplished can we take a deep breath and speak truth to them — truth about how we have taken on the habits of spiritual toughness and why. This truth, however, must remain focused on ourselves rather than become a weapon to coerce them into changing their lives into something resembling ours. Our only obligation to them is to be truth-tellers. Whether they change as a result of hearing this truth is an issue between them and God.

Our ability to be patient with others finds its greatest success whenever we remind ourselves it is not our job to ensure those others are conducting their faith-life in the manner they should be. God reserves this judgment for himself. Frankly, we have enough on our plate to worry about. Practicing patience helps us to keep this truth in focus.

The world provides no help in our desire to be more patient.

There is a concept in Christian doctrine called "sanctification." In the Reformed Christian Tradition of which I am part, The Westminster Confession of Faith has this to say about it:

"They who are effectually called and regenerated, having a new heart and a new spirit created in them, are further sanctified [made holy]... through the virtue of Christ's death and resurrection, by his Word and Spirit dwelling in them... This sanctification is throughout the whole [person], yet imperfect in this life: there [is] still some remnants of corruption in every part... yet, through the continual supply of strength from the sanctifying Spirit of Christ, the [sins are] overcome: and so the saints grow in grace, perfecting holiness in the fear of God" (The Westminster Confession of Faith, Sections 6.075 - 6.077); [bracketed words are mine].[9]

Do we hear the part about the growth in our relationship with God being "imperfect in this life?" The Westminster Confession of Faith was written in 1646... in England. This means a bunch of stiff upper-lipped, stodgy, British churchmen understood almost four hundred years ago the importance of being patient with both ourselves and with other people.

We are blessed inasmuch as they did not live in a world of either instant oatmeal or instant messaging. We are not blessed inasmuch as we do live in such a fast-paced world. The speed of just about everything around us is one more aspect of our environment which works against our desire to be more patient.

The world we inhabit is not at all concerned about pausing to allow anything to catch up with its aspirations. The men who wrote The Westminster Confession of Faith lived at a time when it was easier to habituate patience because life was lived at a slower pace. This means we must be more intentional in our pausing than they were in theirs. So, draw a deep breath, let it out slowly, and be reminded of this: patience is the first characteristic of love, and God is love and patience — among his other holy attributes — personified.

Cultivating patience demonstrates to God we trust him more now than we have been.

Cultivating patience is my tenth habit of spiritual toughness because placing it here helps to end this literary journey where it began: by talking about how we have a difficult time trusting God. Nobody trusts him; just like not one of us is good enough within ourselves to exist in his presence. In other words, don't feel too bad about not trusting God — the rest of us are right there with you.

Now, we may not be able to trust God perfectly, but we sure as heck can trust him more than we do now. This is where being a patient child of God becomes important for us. When we habituate patience — to

111

ourselves or to others — we demonstrate to God our growing trust in his plans for us.

God has already charted our life's course. God knows our life has been filled with hardship and sin. Furthermore, he has given us many opportunities — through events both good and bad — for us to stop punishing ourselves and to accept his unconditional love through the death and resurrection of Jesus Christ. Accepting this truth also means accepting God has won for us that complete, unassailable, and final victory over every bad decision we have ever made.

It is easier to be patient when we remember God has rigged the plan for humanity's salvation in our favor. But, it takes a spiritually tough person to believe it and live out this belief every day instead of trying to come up with his or her own scheme by way of spiritual strength. My fervent hope is for each of us to become this hard-as-nails, rough-riding, tough child of God we intuitively knew we both wanted and needed to be.

12

Concluding Thoughts

The student masters the habits of spiritual toughness by becoming the teacher.

If this book has had any impact, about now you may feel embarrassed or perhaps angry at the realization of having lived and done and decided about your faith in God all the while using the world's strength-language. No one likes to admit the way he or she has been doing something is ineffective. Believe me when I say I am right there with you. And when that *something* is our faith-life, those feelings are amplified. If you find yourself harboring the same sort of shame after reading this book which I felt after writing it, consider that shame to be a blessing. If you are in any way like me, perhaps we are both finally ready to embrace the change in how to live a spiritually tough rather than a spiritually strong life.

The purpose of this book has been to serve as an introduction to a way for all people of faith — but for Christians in particular — to go about forging a faith-life with which they can be satisfied. It is not intended to be (nor is it in any manner) an all-encompassing guide to a person's spiritual journey.

What counts is how the person of faith handles these habits of spiritual toughness: how much he or she believes in them; how successfully she incorporate them into her daily living; and how far he is willing to model these habits to those closest to him.

For the near-term, we may be able to count ourselves only as apprentices when it comes to the practice of these spiritual habits. And that is fine because we all have a great deal of unlearning to do. The influences of the world's strength-language have been applied to us like those layers of paint and wallpaper on the kitchen walls of my grandmother's house. The old self has to be stripped away before the new self can become.[1]

Being a student of the habits of spiritual toughness is the discipline of stripping away these old, worthless ideas about how faith in God is supposed to operate. One day, we will discover most, if not all, these new habits are a natural part of our daily walk with God. The change may be gradual or it may come like a bolt of lightning, but the moment we embark on this rebooted faith journey, be assured, that change will come.

Then the student has the opportunity to become the teacher. When we find ourselves in the place of being able to give intelligent answers to someone else's questions about the habits of spiritual toughness, we will be able to claim mastery of this old and very biblical way of living out our faith in God. But, mastery is not perfection, nor will it ever lead to that condition in this life. Neither is mastery a sign we have finished being a student of spiritual toughness. It most certainly is not that! For the Christian, what mastery of these habits means is God has given us the opportunity to share in a fresh way the Good News of Jesus' saving grace.

My sources of inspiration gave me a more perceptive ear and eye.

The inspiration for this book came from two very different (and decidedly unbiblical) sources. The first was something I read in Chris

Kyle's book "American Sniper." In it, he wrote about how being a Navy SEAL "is more about mental toughness than anything else."[2] Reading that was like a smack between the eyes. If military elites like Mr. Kyle were placing a premium on mental toughness in the pursuit of their missions, I asked myself why wasn't I focused on spiritual toughness in the pursuit of my own mission work?

The second source of inspiration came from an excerpt in a book I read on the internet from psychotherapist Amy Morin entitled "13 Things Mentally Strong People Don't Do."[3] Many of the chapter headings in my book are one or more of her thirteen points re-worked and melded together into new themes which pertain to a person's faith-life instead of to their mental strength.

While both Mr. Kyle and Ms. Morin get credit for helping me frame my argument, reading the excerpt from her book and his memoir about life as a military sniper only reinforced in my mind how pernicious and pervasive the world's strength-language has become.

In writing this book, I have gained a more perceptive ear and eye to just how deep Christians in particular are wallowing in the scum-pond of strength-language's influence. In reading this book, you may discover something similar. In our minds, there should be only one way to proceed: we must climb out, rinse ourselves off, and find a cleaner pool of ideas in which to immerse ourselves. I believe by cultivating and practicing the habits of spiritual toughness we do this.

And in doing so, we will discover we have become embraced by a deeper sense of spiritual wellbeing. This is not to say our faith-life before we began to habituate spiritual toughness was not something worthwhile. It's just that — as satisfying as our prior faith-life might have been for us — it was burdened by having been immersed in strength-language.

Neither am I suggesting that by adopting the more defensive and reflective habits of spiritual toughness our faith in God has become passive; only that God provides the lion's share of the heavy lifting. As far as our faith goes, we must still make the effort to believe! Like a loving parent, God always reaches out to us in mercy before we reach out to him in faith.[4] Pursuing a life of faith through the habits of spiritual toughness allows us to more easily accept this truth.

I have listed ten habits of spiritual toughness. It is up to you to discover the others.

Finally, even if we each master the ten habits of spiritual toughness presented in this book, please understand there are other habits left for us to discover and incorporate into our faith-life.[5] Think of the habits I have introduced as being like different tools. Almost every household has a hammer and a screwdriver. Not every home has a table saw or other specialized piece of woodworking equipment. God may place before you or me the opportunity to acquire a unique habit of spiritual toughness other people may not need. We must be open to uncovering these other habits and learning how to incorporate them into our daily walk with God — if the way presents itself.

And as you go about doing this, I pray you do so with all the love of our Heavenly Father, all the grace of his Son Jesus Christ, and all the encouragement of the Holy Spirit at your back. Taking-on the habits of spiritual toughness is, I believe, what the apostle Paul meant when he challenged the church in Ephesus to put on God's "full armor." God has given us his own strength so we can be spiritually tough as we weather the storms of life and also bear witness to the truth of his love for us in Christ Jesus, our Lord and Savior.

Believe it. Habituate it. Live it.

Acknowledgments

I would like to express my deep and abiding gratitude to the following persons without whose assistance and support this book could not have been brought to publication: my wife Darlene Truman, my friend and colleague in ministry John Lersch, my editor Terry Hemlinger, Professor Byron Jackson of Pittsburgh Theological Seminary, and the fine people at CreateSpace for readying the manuscript for printing. I appreciate the way each of these folk both challenged me and encouraged me to improve the text.

In addition, I would like to express my sincere appreciation to the congregation of the First Presbyterian Church of Kendallville, Indiana, for their patience as the themes for this book were spread upon their ears each Sunday during the Lenten Season of 2015. They were treated to the unusual (for them) experience of having their pastor actually read aloud his sermons rather than experiencing the extemporaneous deliveries to which they had become accustomed. To the extent this book possesses a coherent voice, it is due to them having to bear the new-born noise of these themes on spiritual toughness before I transformed those sermons into book chapters.

Finally, I give the Holy Spirit ultimate credit for whatever good there may be in this book. The other stuff is entirely my fault.

Notes

Preface

1. Last I checked, there were over sixty pages of books on the Amazon.com™ website alone which will appear to anyone who inputs the phrase spiritual strength into their browser's search engine. Likewise, the electronic catalogue operated by Family Christian™ had over sixteen pages of books on the subject. Clearly, spiritual strength is both a popular and profitable topic.

2. The word strength and its many iterations appears over 300 times in the various English language translations of the Bible. Many different Greek words are used to convey this concept in the New Testament. For example, κράταιός can translate as strong, resistless, or potent. The word δύναμη can mean force, power, or strength; whereas ἰσχυρά is a word which can mean mighty, but which is translated as strong in 1 Corinthians 1:27 of the ESV Bible. The point I am making is that translations of the New Testament inevitably either extend or compress the original meaning of the Greek word in question. This happens because many words contain a cultural component which literally becomes lost in the act of translation. Also — as in the case of the word strength, — there can be a wide spectrum of meaning within a single word. Consequently, English language readers of the Bible must trust that the translator has captured the essence of the author's meaning. If we assume the underlying Greek or Hebrew word being used exactly corresponds to the word which appears in English, we are volunteering to be duped and disappointed. Finally, add to the above this truth: how each of us understands a word like strength is completely unique.

3. An idiom attributed to the French language used to describe a person with a broad base of knowledge yet possessing only a shallow understanding of the subject matter.

Chapter 1: Strength vs Toughness

1. Scripture quotations are from the ESV® Bible (The Holy Bible, English Standard Version®), copyright © 2001 by Crossway, a publishing ministry of Good News Publishers. Used by permission. All rights reserved.

2. In "Lifespan Perspectives on Natural Disasters," a variety of authors explore the spectrum of human emotional and psychological response to Hurricane Katrina and other natural disasters. They collectively seek to discover the underlying qualities which lead to vulnerability in one person while another person experiencing the same event is able to project resiliency.

3. John Calvin, in his seminal work "Institutes of the Christian Religion;" Book 2; Chapter 1; Section 4; p. 245, agrees with Saint Augustine that Adam's chief offense before God was the pride of ambition. This original sin is then reflected by every descendent of Adam in the form of self-admiration: we hold ourselves in a far higher regard than we have any right to claim. To correct this false and fatal sense of self, Calvin would have human beings acknowledge their total depravity before God.

4. Ibid, Book 2; Chapter 1; Section 9; pp. 252-253, where Calvin talks about the apostle Paul's third chapter of The Letter to the Romans and how sin is not some shallow impulse stemming from sensual thinking, but is, in truth, the total corruption of the person down to his or her very soul.

5. The list of people who have died in the pursuit of adventures such as mountaineering, sea kayaking, spelunking, skydiving, or auto racing (just to name a few) is seemingly endless. Nevertheless, the human drive to achieve in spite of obvious danger and death remains undiminished.

6. An Imperial Roman general so feted was — on the day of his triumphal celebration — the top citizen of the Empire, and was permitted many honors and feasts even beyond his life. But Roman stoicism insisted great men be reminded there is a natural limit to all greatness.

7. For the purposes of this book, I am defining strength-language as follows: any way of conceptualizing and communicating our place in the world; any set of standards; or any belief system which seeks to promote, reinforce, and otherwise encourage the boundlessness of human greatness. This concept thereby embodies the antithesis of the Reformed Christian tenet of the total depravity of the person.

8. The axiom, "The best defense is a good offense," is one example of the intimidating power of strength-language. This adage also shows the application of strength can occur from fear of being attacked by our enemies.

9. Here the Greek word translated as strong is ἐνδύναμούσθε, which is a form of the noun δύναμη; often translated into English as power. It is the basis

for the English word dynamo. In the context of Paul's argument, however, he is urging the reader to acquire a particular power essential to having faith in God. As such, it is —according to Paul — a power to be generated more by our brains than by our brawn.

10. Herodotus. "The Histories," Published by Viking Penguin, a member of Penguin Group (USA) LLC, (2014), Book Seven, Pp. 520-530. Used by permission. All rights reserved.

11. Goodwin, Doris Kearns. "The Bully Pulpit," Simon and Schuster Paperbacks, A Division of Simon and Schuster, Inc., (2013), p. 40. Used by permission. All rights reserved.

12. *Ibid*. Used by permission. All rights reserved.

13. *Ibid*. Used by permission. All rights reserved.

Chapter 2: Have the Courage to Embrace Change

1. A list of people in the Bible willing to embrace change also would include the patriarch Joseph and King David from the Old Testament; and the eleven post-resurrection apostles, Saul, and Jesus' brother James from the New Testament. Each one of these was rewarded for his respective ability to embrace change. Judas Iscariot — who could not do so — met a far different fate.

2. In Mark 1:4, the Greek form of this word is μετανοίας, while in the fifteenth verse, it is μετανοείτε. These words — which translate, respectively, as repent and repentance — imply an action of something like a juror being swayed by the weight of evidence in a court case, or, alternately, any person by the logic of a well-made argument the conclusions of which are irrefutable.

3. As a young man, I had the privilege of knowing more than a few veterans of World War II. As they would tell me about being a prisoner of war under the Japanese, or about watching from a transport plane Polish paratroopers falling onto German positions in Holland, or what it was like to be in Bastogne in December of 1944, they all spoke about being afraid and how some soldiers were able to accommodate this fear while others could not. I was told time and again the ones who couldn't often were the first ones to get killed or to die from the elements. I learned quite a lot about fear and courage from these amazing veterans.

4. Maya Angelou. (n.d.). BrainyQuote.com. Retrieved July 28, 2015, from BrainyQuote.com Web site: http://www.brainyquote.com/quotes/quotes/m/mayaangelo120859.html. Used by permission. All rights reserved.

5. Aristotle's understanding of virtue is more nuanced than those mentioned here. He believed human virtue occupied the middle ground between extreme thoughts and actions. As such, even-tempered people were, for him, more virtuous because they were living into their humanity in the best possible way. This is a view I share because it presupposes the universal accessibility of all virtues.

6. The only characteristic absent from Jesus' humanity was the quality of sin. In both Romans 5 and 1 Corinthians 15:23, the apostle Paul describes Christ as the new Adam — excepting whereas through the first human all humanity is bound to sin and death, through Jesus, those who believe on his name and sacrifice are bound to life. In order to provide this gift, the Christ of God would have to be as holy as God.

7. The concept known as entropy can be understood in two ways: the change in entropy in a closed system is represented in equations by the symbol (ΔS), while absolute entropy (S) is missing the mathematical symbol for change, the delta (Δ). Absolute entropy is understood as a statistical mechanism for expressing the lack of information within a given system. For reasons like this, entropy has become a common means of understanding chaos and disorder within systems.

8. Goodwin, Doris Kearns. "The Bully Pulpit," Simon and Schuster Paperbacks, A Division of Simon and Schuster, Inc., (2013), p. 40. Used by permission. All rights reserved.

Chapter 3: Learn How to Manage Life

1. At one point in writing this book, I tried to find some middle ground between the competing concepts of control and management; in one instance, imagining taking control of one's life within the limitations of human sin. But even a cursory testing-out of this idea led me to the sad conclusion it resembled something like poorly assembled taxidermy rather than a viable third way between these diametrically opposed philosophies.

2. Korda, Michael. "With Wings Like Eagles: The Untold Story of the Battle of Britain" Success Research Corporation, an imprint of HarperCollins Publishers, 2010, p. 34. Used by permission. All rights reserved.

3. *Ibid*, p. 37. Used by permission. All rights reserved.

4. *Ibid*, p. 284. Used by permission. All rights reserved.

5. Gerstacker, Diana. "How Lindsey Vonn Recovered from a Devastating Knee Injury," *The Active Times*. Posted on January 28, 2015, 6:00 pm. Used by permission.

6. Dwayne King's book "Control Your Destiny" and Kay Porter's work "The Mental Athlete" are but two volumes among scores which advocate for the budding athlete to take control of his or her physical development and athletic disciplines. The realm of sports is also where the vast majority of books have been written which focus on the subject of mental toughness.

7. Jack Nicklaus. (n.d.). BrainyQuote.com. Retrieved July 29, 2015, from BrainyQuote.com Web site: http://www.brainyquote.com/quotes/quotes/j/jacknickla585794.htm. Used by permission.

Chapter 4: Covet God's Call

1. One iconic story of covetousness involving Naboth's vineyard is found in 1 Kings 21:1-16. Two which come to mind about money are Luke 22:3-6 (Judas Iscariot's betrayal of Jesus for 30 pieces of silver) and Acts 5:1-11 (Ananias and Sapphira withholding their wealth). The two tales in Genesis about Abram/Abraham lying about his true relationship to Sarai/Sarah with Pharaoh and Abimelech, (respectively, Genesis 12:10-20 and 20:1-19) are stories more about this patriarch's cunning sense of self-preservation than about the covetousness of these two clueless monarchs.

2. Kohlberg, Lawrence. "Essays on Moral Development, Vol. 1: The Philosophy of Moral Development" Harper & Row, 1981, p. 17. Used by permission.

3. *Ibid*, p. 412. Used by permission.

4. Called many things from morality tale to myth, "Lord of the Flies" by William Golding, is for me an allegory on the destructive inclinations possible in any tribal culture whether said culture is technological or agrarian in nature or, indeed, anything in between.

5. To his enduring credit, Nietzsche's conceptualizations of the super-human did not include the murdering of those who were mentally or physically incapacitated. Quite to the contrary, he saw illness as something which had societal value. The Nazis alone tried to justify the extermination of over eleven million Europeans by suggesting it was the merciful act of putting political prisoners, Jews, Poles, Slovaks, Roma, and the developmentally disabled out of their respective miseries.

6. Edwards, Tyron. "The New Dictionary of Thoughts: A Cyclopedia of Quotations," Kindle Edition. (2015), pp. 114-115. Used by permission. All rights reserved.

7. God's holy omnipotence is derived from his changeless moral character. God cannot be false either to himself or to his creation. That the universe exists is not merely evidence of the truthfulness of God, but its proof. When God speaks, his words are always true. This veracity is the basis of so-called Natural Law upon which the universe exists. When we conform our thinking, acting, and speaking to God's revealed word, we also speak truth. Pilate's question, on the other hand, reflected his own belief in the subjective nature of truth, and was rhetorical. Ironically, Jesus stood before Pilate as the physical embodiment of God's eternal and unchanging truth.

8. Bull Durham (1988). Metro-Goldwyn-Mayer Studios, Inc. All rights reserved.

9. The word which translates into the English language as satan is not a proper name; rather a direct phonetic transfer from the original Hebrew word השטן, which means the adversary. Evil is anything adversarial to God and/or his creation. Especially evil is the toxic mind-set which leads to self-hatred.

Chapter 5: Draw Lessons From the Past

1. Callahan, Maureen. "The Brutal Secrets Behind 'The Biggest Loser,'" New York Post online edition, posted on January 18, 2015, 7:00 am. Used by permission. All rights reserved.

2. In both economics and game theory, a zero-sum game is the name for any closed system whereby a change in the gain or loss of some asset by one player is balanced by a corresponding loss or gain by another player or players within that same system. Let us say the asset in question is a cherry pie and there are ten people who want a piece of it. In a zero-sum game, the dimensions of the pie never changes. Therefore, if one person takes for himself a slice two-tenths in size, at least one person among the rest of the players must contend with less than one-tenth of a slice. In a non zero-sum game, the dimensions of the asset might expand to permit every player to obtain as much pie as he or she wished to have.

3. For me, there has never been depicted a better visual metaphor for failure at maintaining control of our lives than the image of uncountable specters shooting through the roof of a broken-down building. The irony, of course, is while this scene appears to be a disaster, it is actually the first step in the resolution of the underlying problem: Gozer the Destroyer's return. The process is the same for the individual: Only when we admit our frailty to God (confess

our demons) are we able to take advantage of the healing power of God's amazing grace which is able to defeat them.

4. Stress-Inoculation Training and Exposure Therapy are but two of many strategies clinical psychologists and psychotherapists use to help a person suffering from post-traumatic stress learn how to recall the details of the event or events without reliving them. Both techniques ask the person to not keep traumatic memories bottled up.

5. Mr. Musk's many Twitter™ comments are usually as informative as they are amusing.

6. One of the final lines laconically delivered by actor Desmond Llewelyn in the movie The World is Not Enough (1999) by Eon Productions.

7. For a more thorough treatment of the importance of Joseph's story to the Christian's understanding of the power of redemption through love, you may wish to read "Joseph and the Gospel of Many Colors: Reading an Old Story in a New Way," by Voddie Baucham, Jr., (2013), Crossway, a publishing ministry of Good News Publishers.

8. There is no better commentary on this and many other extraordinary acts of mercy from aggrieved persons toward an enemy than John S. Dickerson's guest editorial in the June 22, 2015, edition of USA Today.

Chapter 6: Feel Gratitude Instead of Entitlement

1. Patterson, Brianna. "Why our Obsession with the Rich and Famous is a Cultural Dead End," *The Diamondback*, The University of Maryland's Independent Student Newspaper; Diversions, Arts; posted on Wednesday, February 19, 2014, 1:00 am.

2. Commager, Henry Steel. "The American Mind: An Interpretation of American Thought and Character Since the 1880s" Yale University Press, 1950, p. 210.

3. Translated into English, *laissez-faire* means to "let us/them go." In the context of economic exchange, a more appropriate translation would be to say, "Let us do whatever we want to do." At its heart, it is an economic system which rejects most third-party regulations (from governments, for example), but instead believes the individuals making a particular transaction should be free to make whatever deals they can with no outside interference.

4. Commager, Henry Steel. "The American Mind: An Interpretation of American Thought and Character Since the 1880s" Yale University Press, 1950, p. 209.

5. *Ibid,* p. 215.

6. *Sola fide* (faith alone) is Latin for one of Reformed Christianity's major tenets: the idea that the Christian is justified (made right) before God only through his or her faith in Jesus Christ. Nothing else — including so-called good works — matters.

7. What I am calling acceptance should not be confused with the philosophy of fatalism. A person who is fatalistic by nature is often governed by negative expectations. One example of this mind-set is the phrase: "Expect the worst, but hope for the best." Under the guise of acceptance, that phrase might look like this: "Hope always for God's goodness, but welcome whatever comes as a challenge to be overcome by faith."

8. Often described by the phrase, "The sum is greater than its constituent parts." synergy — from the Greek word συνεργός which means "to work together" — is a widely seen phenomena in nature from biology to physics. It may also be seen in human endeavors as varied as psychology and business. Spiritual synergy is nothing more than the recognition the various aspects of Christian faith often work in concert to reinforce and uphold one another.

9. More books have been written on prayer than on probably any other human activity other than eating food. There are far too many great books on prayer in print than space here to list even a small fraction of them. I will say one of my favorite authors in this area is Douglas V. Steere. I enjoy reading his work "Dimensions of Prayer." Others who have written well on the subject include (in no particular order); Max Lucado, Thomas Keating, Philip Yancey, and Helen Steiner Rice. Any of these authors — and scores more beyond — will be able to teach you more about prayer than I.

10. One technique I discovered in my youth was to imagine myself taking a few steps out of the center of the crisis I was in the midst of in order to take up the vantage of an outside observer. My goal in doing this was to take on a more objective perspective of the given situation. This simple technique permitted me to more clearly see the conflict from multiple points-of-view — including that of the person with whom I was in conflict. I also discovered my emotionality often became detached or muted as a result. This gave me the opportunity to ask if my emotions were part of the problem or part of the solution.

Chapter 7: Risk it All

1. Faith in God — far from being an irrational decision — is ideally a response based upon a careful and sober examination of the available evidence. Unchecked preconceptions and other biases may skew a person's perception of this evidence and his or her subsequent conclusions. Read Acts 2:1-41 for an example of this. Here, the event of the outpouring of God's Holy Spirit is interpreted (perceived) by some as drunkenness, whereas the apostle Peter translates this strange happening as the fulfillment of a prophecy spoken by the prophet Joel. Faith in God can indeed be a powerful filter on reality which is able to alter our perception of the information our senses provide our brains. In other words: believing can lead to seeing. But so too can seeing sometimes lead to believing. Therefore, my use of the word optics is entirely appropriate in this context since it calls attention to Mr. Spielberg's use of an optical illusion to demonstrate the danger of an unchecked perspective.

2. For a more detailed examination of the literary value of the Bible, please read an essay by Professor Jan Haluska of Southern Adventist University entitled, "The Bible and Literature" (2000). All rights reserved. Ultimately, the Bible qualifies as literature because it fits Italo Calvino's oft-quoted definition of a classical work: "A classic is a book that has never finished saying what it has to say."

3. Dialogue spoken by actor Rowan Witt in The Matrix (1999), produced by Village Roadshow Pictures. Used by permission. All rights reserved.

4. Babbel, Susan. (2011). "Fear of Success"; *Psychology Today* © 1991-2015 Sussex Publishers, LLC. Used by permission. All rights reserved.

5. Conceived by Lawrence J. Peter in his book, "The Peter Principle: Why Things Always Go Wrong" (1969), it was intended as an evaluative tool in deciding which managerial candidates would no longer be promoted based on their current success rather than on how well their skill set matched the position for which they were being considered.

6. This theme is expertly explored by H. Richard Niebuhr in his classic book, "Christ and Culture" (Reissued 2001); Harper San Francisco, a Division of Harper Collins Publishers. All rights reserved.

7. A classic straw-man fallacy is where the proposition from one debater is modified by his opponent who then argues against the now false, but similar proposition instead of against the original proposition.

Chapter 8: Be Spiritually Fed

1. Jean Anthelme Brillat-Savarin — a late eighteenth to early nineteenth century French politician better known for his love of and commentary on French gourmet cuisine — was the originator of the concept.

2. The many English language translations of the Bible available to the modern reader can give the impression of a work which is well-established by original source material. In reality, we do not have access to a single original text for any book of the Bible. Instead, we have tens of thousands of scrolls and fragments of scrolls — some of which are very old. Together, they provide a high degree of confidence that what we read in our translations is both authoritative and sufficient when it comes to our understanding of what God is saying to us.

3. One example of a textual dispute is found at the end of The Gospel of Mark. Most modern Biblical scholars agree the best textual witnesses place the end of this book at Mark 16:8. And yet, many English translations of Mark will include Mark 16:9-20, with verse twenty being the last one. Should this dispute be for us a source of worry or doubt? No. What this tells me is that from the beginning, people were trying to interpret the meaning of the words they were reading; something any modern reader of the Bible is expected to do.

4. Williamson, Sam. "What is Spiritual Malnutrition?" Beliefs of the Heart Blog. April 9, 2013. Used by permission. All rights reserved.

5. The very first action in the traditional Alcoholics' Anonymous Twelve-Step Program is for the addict to admit he or she cannot control or even manage this illness.

6. Although it is impossible to attribute this saying to a particular person, Henry Kett, in an 1814 collection of writings entitled "The Flowers of Wit, or a Choice Collection of *Bon Mots*," apparently became one of the first persons to set this particular proverb to print.

7. Some of the better textual witnesses place the first use of the "man's" formal name at Genesis 3:17. The woman's name is first mentioned in Genesis 3:20, where Adam is credited with giving it to her and explains why she is to be called Eve.

8. Just do the math: if a person breathes between 14 and 17 times a minute, and there are 60 minutes in an hour and 24 hours in a day, that works out to be from 20,160 to 24,480 breaths per day. The average of those two numbers is 22,320.

9. Coleman III, Thomas J. and Koenig, Dr. Harold G. "Religion, Spirituality and Health - An Interview with Dr. Harold Koenig." The Religious Studies Project. Podcast from March 24, 2014. Used by permission. All rights reserved.

10. The formal term is anal retentiveness though it is no longer widely used by psychologists. Still, I have seen how difficult it is for a developmentally delayed young man to become successfully toilet trained.

11. Donne, John. "Devotions upon Emergent Occasions" Meditation XVII. 1624. Used by permission.

Chapter 9: Encourage and Enjoy the Success of Others

1. Men — though at far less frequent rates — also may be susceptible to the effects of a controlling spouse or partner. Jealousy and its twin emotion envy are rooted in the world's strength-language and arise when the false notion of a person's superiority clashes with the reality of a better idea or success coming from their partner. Because of their reliance on strength-language, those who seek to control have trouble discarding their envy. Jealous people, instead, often resolve this inner conflict through the physical, mental, and/or emotional domination of their partner. Having thus reestablished (at least in their own minds) their superiority, the ideas and accomplishments of the other person can be more easily discounted or altogether ignored.

2. The amazing story of Mary Kay Ash's success can be read in any number of books. Some of the ones she herself authored include: "Miracles Happen" by Mary Kay Ash, published by William Morrow (2003); "Mary Kay: The Success Story of America's Most Dynamic Businesswoman" by Mary Kay Ash, published by Harper-Collins, Rev. Sub. Edition (1987); and "Mary Kay" by Mary Kay Ash, published by Harper-Collins (1981).

3. Mary Kay Ash. (2015). The Biography.com website. Retrieved 04:25, Aug 19, 2015, from http://www.biography.com/people/mary-kay-ash-197044. Used by permission.

4. *Ibid.*

5. I am referring here to the various waves of colonialism which have swept over the world beginning in antiquity with the Egyptians, Persians, Greeks, and Phoenicians, and continuing until the modern era with the French, Dutch, Germans, Russians, Japanese, English, and Americans. Colonialism always carries within it an element of paternalism which gives the conquering group justification to dominate the indigenous population because so-called primitive peoples need to be provided the trappings of civilization.

6. Executive Committee of the American Anti-Slavery Committee, Slavery and the International Slave Trade in the United States of America, London: Thomas Ward And Co. 1841. Anti-Slavery collection. Question 26. All rights reserved.

7. This very thing happened in a community where my wife and I have resided.

8. Bundy, Cliven. As quoted in an interview with the New York Times on April 23, 2014. Used by permission. All rights reserved.

9. Please read Matthew 25:31-46, for an especially pertinent — and chilling — expansion of this idea.

Chapter 10: Love the Unlovable

1. For example, persons diagnosed with schizoid personality disorder may not be able to exhibit any kind of emotionality — either positive or negative.

2. For us to feel hatred is not, in and of itself, a sin. It is what we do with that hate which matters. Even when Jesus (in Matthew 5:22) talks about "everyone who is angry with his brother will be liable to judgment," such a person first has to move from emotions to thoughts. My interpretation of Jesus' point is this: there is no difference between impure actions and impure thinking, not that feelings themselves have an intrinsically moral quality.

3. Practical considerations alone dictate we initially be suspicious of and perhaps even hostile toward strangers or rivals. It is safer for us to begin with hate and then move toward more generous feelings once our suspicions have been assuaged. So, far from this being a moral judgment, it is the simple observation that most people on this planet are wary creatures.

4. Acts 7:60.

5. Acts 7:52.

6. Most big-ticket purchases come with what is called a limited warranty: that is, the manufacturer limits the time-frame or the amount of any refund by which the object can be either repaired or replaced. The guarantee Sears™ used to give on the tools they sold, on the other hand, is very much like God's unconditional love toward us. It used to be possible to take in any damaged Craftsman™ tool and the staff would hand you a replacement free of charge and no questions asked. I did this in 1978 with a crescent wrench I accidentally dropped ten feet onto concrete.

7. Read Deuteronomy 11:26-28, for an example of the contractual structure of God's covenants with Israel.

Chapter 11: Cultivate Patience

1. This definition of patience comes from my years in service as a pastor and from my own failures and successes at being patient.

2. Patience is not inactivity and neither is it passive. Ideally, patience is the conscious choice to refrain from all other possible actions. Take for example one of the most important rules concerning a lifeguard's rescue of a drowning swimmer: they are instructed never to attempt the rescue of someone who is flailing, but are to wait until the swimmer tires himself out before placing him in the proper hold and swimming him to safety. This pause on the lifeguard's part can mean the difference between a successful rescue and a double drowning.

3. Even a cursory reading of the Bible informs us God exists outside the ebb and flow of time and space. Since God is not bound by these limitations, his perspective is one of perfect patience (among all of God's other perfect qualities). Our choice to be patient, while never perfect, can give us a brief taste of this perspective; much like stepping into the room in Independence Hall where the Declaration of Independence was signed can impart a sense of grandeur beyond what may be gleaned from a history book.

4. There is a fine line which separates teaching someone a thing and doing the learning for them. The person who refuses to learn for himself cannot be aided by our taking-in double portions of knowledge and hoping he comes by enlightenment through some form of osmosis. The same is true for faith in God: each of us is responsible for our own salvation.

5. The classical summation of Sir Isaac Newton's Third Law of Motion outlined in his great opus, "Philosophiæ Naturalis Principia Mathematica" (1687).

6. From "Newton's Laws - Lesson 4 - Newton's Third Law of Motion; The Physics Classroom" (2015); by Tom Henderson, Glenbrook High School in Glenview, IL. Used by permission. All rights reserved.

7. Exodus 21:24.

8. Romans 4:15.

9. John Calvin, in his "Institutes of the Christian Religion" Book 3, Chapter 14, Section 4, p. 771, reminds the Christian that, "...there is no sanctification apart from communion with Christ," In other words, it's impossible for us to attain holiness without God's assistance.

Chapter 12: Concluding Thoughts

1. For the theological foundation of this statement, please read the apostle Paul's Letter to the Romans; Chapter 6. In it, Paul speaks directly to this need.

2. Kyle, Chris. "American Sniper," William Marrow; An Imprint of HarperCollins Publishers, 2014, p. 29. Used by permission. All rights reserved.

3. Morin, Amy. "13 Things Mentally Strong People Don't Do," William Marrow; An Imprint of HarperCollins Publishers, 2014. All rights reserved.

4. Please read Psalm 139 for a most excellent example of this truth.

5. A good place to begin identifying these other habits of spiritual toughness is to read 1 Corinthians 12:1-11. Based on this Pauline passage, some examples of specialized habits might include fasting, healing, generosity, and prophesy. Yet, even Paul could not exhaust all possible habits; as it is my belief God can and does create new ones to fit the times in which we live.

www.ingramcontent.com/pod-product-compliance
Lightning Source LLC
Chambersburg PA
CBHW020910090426
42736CB00008B/559